THE HISTORY OF THE
NHRA
Winternationals

ISBN: 0-9842043-1-8

THE HISTORY OF THE NHRA WINTERNATIONALS

A snow-capped mountain backdrop. New cars. Fresh paint. Sponsorship launches. Rookie debuts. Memorable moments. Incredible upsets. Together, they mean only one thing to drag racing fans the world over: the NHRA Winternationals.

Since 1960, the first official rumble of high-performance engines has echoed across Fairplex at Pomona in Southern California, signaling not just the beginning of another year of exciting drag racing, but also the launch of a thousand dreams of glory. Sometimes a chill reminiscent of the event name may be in the air — snow even dusted the ground beneath the palm trees one year — but the racing is always scorching hot.

As the annual kickoff of NHRA's racing schedule, the Winternationals is closely watched by fans everywhere, not just the knowledgeable fans who pack the grandstands eager for their first whiffs of nitromethane after the off-season. From Don Garlits' first winged dragster in 1963 or his revolutionary rear-engine Top Fueler in 1971 to Bill Jenkins' tube-framed Vega Pro Stocker and Kenny Bernstein's aerodynamically enhanced Budweiser Kings, the Winternationals has proven a fertile ground for the birth of new technologies as well as the launchpad for up-and-coming drivers to stake their claims at one of drag racing's most majestic events.

In 2010, the Winternationals will celebrate its golden anniversary. In these pages, you'll relive the excitement and wonder of every Winternationals and explore in-depth the many facets of the event's intriguing history, from the heroes of the track to the machines they rode to glory.

In its five decades on the NHRA calendar, the Winternationals probably has produced 100 years worth of memories for the faithful who flock each year to Pomona. On these two pages are 25 of the most memorable moments from the Winternationals, the order of which will be determined in an online poll. Moments 6 through 25 will be revealed in reverse order on NHRA.com in the weeks before the 2010 event, and the top five will be announced during race week, culminating with the unveiling of the top moment during Sunday's pre-race festivities at the 50th annual event.

1963, Garlits Goes Big
Don Garlits already was a drag racing legend, but his first NHRA win, with a revolutionary and controversial winged Top Fuel dragster, really puts him on the map

1963, The Mystery Train
Bob Muravez, forbidden by his parents to drag race, wins Top Gas in the fabled Freight Train twin-engine dragster using the pseudonym Floyd Lippencott Jr.

1965-66, Hawaiian Domination
Car owner Roland Leong wins Top Fuel back to back, giving Don Prudhomme his first win in 1965 and Mike Snively his a year later

1966, Ladies Day
Shirley Shahan becomes the first woman to win a major drag racing national event eliminator title with her stunning victory in the popular Top Stock class

1968, Galloping Ponies
Ford crashes Mopar's Stocker monopoly with a fleet of 10 Cobra Jet Mustangs, and Al Joniec, at the wheel of the Rice-Holman entry, collects the victory

1969, The Flyin' Hawaiian
Roland Leong's first Hawaiian Funny Car, an ill-handling, full-size Dodge Charger driven by Larry Reyes, takes flight and sails backward through the finish-line lights. The duo wins the race the following year

1970, 'Grumpy' Rules First Pro Stock Go
Crowd favorite Bill Jenkins wins NHRA's first Pro Stock title, besting the previously unbeatable Sox & Martin team in the final with low e.t. of the meet

1971, Garlits Kicks 'em in the Rear
A year after a near-career-ending accident, Don Garlits wins Top Fuel with a revolutionary rear-engine dragster in its NHRA national event debut

1974, Roll Over, Ivo
Tommy Ivo barrel-rolls his beautiful Top Fuel dragster in the finish-line lights during qualifying in a fiery and car-destroying crash

1975, Garlits' Gift
Don Garlits smokes the tires against Don Ewald in round one of Top Fuel, but Ewald is disqualified for crossing the centerline. Garlits wins the event and season title and admits that had he not won the Winternationals, he likely would not have pursued the championship

1975, In Hindsight ...
Dennis Geisler calls his rare rear-engine Funny Car Hindsight; after he backflips the flopper in a huge starting-line wheelstand, he might have had second thoughts on its design

1978, The Real Winternationals
Southern California is supposed to be home to sunshine and blue skies, but the 1978 event is besieged by foul weather, including a rare dusting of snow

1981, The Texas Chainsaw Massacre
The roof of Raymond Beadle's famed Blue Max Funny Car blows off at the finish line on a winning semifinal run, but fellow Texan Kenny Bernstein allows Beadle to saw the roof off of his car and graft it to the Max. Beadle loses the final but not for lack of effort

1982, Seven Seconds to Glory

After years of using a complicated weight-break rule, NHRA switches Pro Stock to a straight-up 500-cubic-inch limit. The big horsepower gains lead to the class' first seven-second pass, by the late Lee Shepherd

1984-85, Thar She Blows (again)!

Al Segrini wins dramatic back-to-back Funny Car titles. In 1984, he rides out a huge top-end blower explosion; the following year, he crosses the finish line with a cockpit full of sparks from a disintegrating clutch

1986, Too Slick for Its Own Good

Gary Ormsby unveils a super-swoopy streamliner, and the car's debut is a bang ... in the worst way. An ignition short caused by the engine-cloaking body leads to a huge blower explosion in the water box on its first pass

1987, The America's Cup, Quarter-Mile Style

While U.S. sailors battle the Australians in the America's Cup, American Kenny Bernstein and Aussie Graeme Cowin wage their own war in Funny Car, complete with flags on their tow vehicles

1989, Up, Up, and Away

Eddie "the Thrill" Hill lives up to his nickname after a front-spoiler malfunction sends his yellow Top Fuel dragster soaring across the finish line

1990, Upset of the Decade

With the ink practically still wet on his nitro license, K.C. Spurlock wins Funny Car in his Pro debut, knocking off John Force, Bruce Larson, and, in the final, Ed "the Ace" McCulloch

1993, 'The King' Gets Crowned

Kenny Bernstein loses more than the Top Fuel final to Joe Amato. The former world champ loses, in succession, an engine, a tire, control of his race car, and the race car itself in a violent top-end tumble that leaves "the Bud King" dazed but unhurt

1997, Scelzi Sez ... Winner

Gary Scelzi wins at his first event since taking the wheel of Alan Johnson's dragster five months after the death of Alan's brother, Blaine. He becomes the first driver since K.C. Spurlock in 1990 to win in his Pro debut

1998, 'The Snake's' Double Strike

The two fuel cars owned by Don "the Snake" Prudhomme double up with wins by Larry Dixon and Ron Capps. Prudhomme hasn't won as a driver or owner in Pomona since 1978

2001, Rookies Rule

Former Top Alcohol Dragster racer Darrell Russell joins Gary Scelzi and K.C. Spurlock as the only drivers to score in their Professional debuts by winning aboard Joe Amato's Top Fuel dragster with rookie crew chief Jimmy Walsh

2006, That's Really Showing 'em

Robert Hight's Funny Car engine blows in round two, destroying the body. The team pulls the body off its show car and wins

2008, The Kid Is All Right

Former Pro Stock Motorcycle racer Antron Brown shows that he is as adept on four wheels as on two when he qualifies No. 1 in his Top Fuel debut

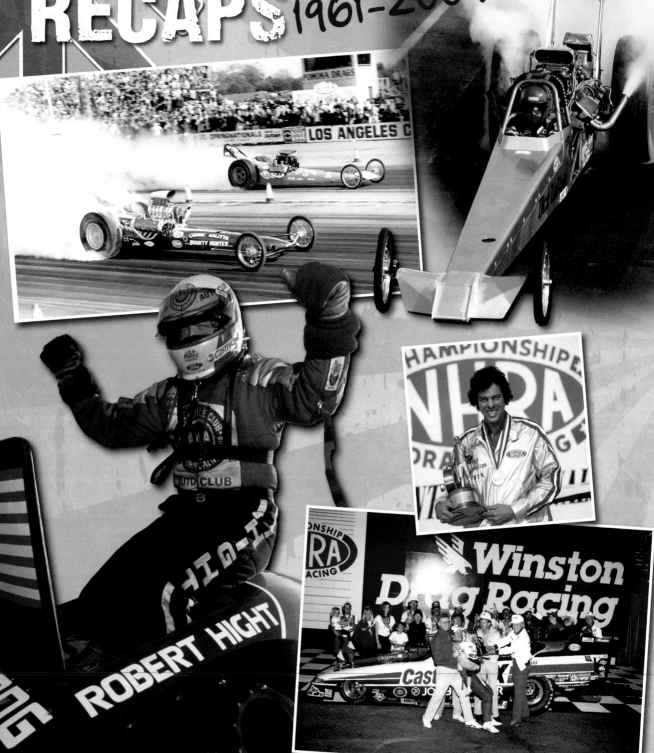

WINTERNATIONALS RECAPS 1961-2009

CHRISMAN WINS INAUGURAL EVENT

The 1961 Winternationals was significant for several reasons. Not only did it join the NHRA Nationals, which was first contested in 1955, as the second event of major stature, but it also gave racers from the West Coast, known as the birthplace of hot rodding, a national event of their own.

The famed Jack Chrisman enjoyed a significant moment in his historic career by scoring Top Eliminator honors with the twin-Chevy-powered Howard Cam Special owned by Jerry Johansen. Chrisman earned his spot in the final by winning the AA/D class competition, and he faced off against A/D class winner Tom McEwen in Dick Rea's single-engine Chevy-powered A/D. Chrisman saved his best for last and scored with low e.t. of the meet, 8.99.

Easily the most ambitious campaigner at the 1961 Winternationals was Mickey Thompson, who fielded five dragsters and several Stockers, all of which were Pontiac-powered. After claiming X/D class honors with his Pontiac Tempest four-cylinder-powered entry, Thompson triumphed in the Middle eliminator final by defeating the highly respected Hirshfield-Buky B/Altered Fiat with a 10.50, 131.

Dick Manz and Johnny Loper earned a place in history as the first Pomona winners of two of the other major titles, in the Little and Street eliminators, respectively.

But perhaps the biggest cheers from the grandstands were for Stock winner Don Nicholson, who showcased the power potential of Chevrolet's then-new 360-horsepower, 409-cid engine by winning from a field of nearly 50 Stockers. Frank Sanders, whose 409 Chevy was tuned by Nicholson, won Super Stock class eliminations Saturday to face Nicholson, the winner of Sunday's Stock eliminator runoffs. Nicholson took the win with a 13.59, 105.88.

In addition, tremendous performances were turned in during the wild three days of competition; 41 new national records were set. Chrisman led the way by eclipsing his AA/D elapsed time of 9.07 with a 9.00, and Jim Nelson set a new AA/D speed mark with a run of 174.92 mph that bettered the 172.08 set by Art Arfons' Allison-powered dragster in Detroit in 1959. Top speed of the meet was a 176-plus-mph clocking, interestingly posted by Hayden Proffitt in the Bayer-Frietas twin-Chevy dragster. Proffitt, of course, would later become famous with his hard-running Super Stock and Funny Car entries.

The Jack Chrisman-driven Howard Cam Special twin-Chevy entry, pictured being fired with the then-traditional push-start ritual, claimed Top Eliminator honors at the first Big Go West.

(Above) The starting line featured a banner with the logo of the Uptown Pomona Lions Club, which with the Pomona Valley Timing Association helped stage the race. (Below) The innovative Mickey Thompson was open to all forms of high-performance engine combinations, and he won Middle eliminator with this four-banger-powered X/Dragster.

(Left) NHRA's Jack Hart worked closely with racers throughout the weekend to ensure a smoothly run inaugural major West Coast event. (Below) Dick Manz not only drove the BM/SP Devin entry owned by Larry Sanchez to Little eliminator honors, but he also set two new national records.

1962

Top Eliminator winner Jim Nelson, left, received a certificate for a new Ford 406-cid engine from Ken Roggy of the Ford Dealers Association, which sponsored the award.

The AA/GD team from Hawaii, with Roland Leong, third from left, and driver Danny Ongais, fourth from left, earned the Best Appearing Crew and Long Distance awards.

Pete Robinson received his e.t. slip for his 8.50 performance, which tied him with Glen Ward and the Howard Cam Special for low e.t. of the meet honors.

After winning his second consecutive Winternationals Stock title, Don Nicholson took his 409 Chevy to the East Coast, where he was much in demand for match race action.

For his first of three Winternationals titles, Hugh Tucker scored in Little eliminator with his A/Street Roadster, which was powered by a genuine Oldsmobile powerplant.

NELSON'S DRAGMASTER DART REIGNS SUPREME

Those who attended the inaugural NHRA Winternationals in 1961 couldn't have helped but notice the huge increase in entries from all parts of the country for the second edition of the Big Go West. Though most of the competitors at the first Winternationals were from the West Coast, the next race attracted the likes of Pete Robinson from Atlanta, Connie Kalitta from Ypsilanti, Mich., and Dave Strickler from York, Pa., as well as many other out-of-state contestants. In just one year, the fledgling Winternationals had gained true national event status.

But in the end, a pair of racers from the West Coast still nabbed the biggest prizes: Jim Nelson of Carlsbad, Calif., won Top Eliminator with his Dodge-powered Dragmaster Dart, and Pasadena, Calif.'s "Dyno Don" Nicholson won Stock for the second year in a row, this time with his new 409-cid '62 Chevy.

Nelson reached the Top Eliminator final after defeating 1961 winner Jack Chrisman in the Dragmaster Straight Arrow entry with an 8.61 in the semi's. One round earlier, Nelson had turned back Kalitta with a solid 8.62. Nelson's foe in the trophy dash was none other than 1961 runner-up Tom McEwen in the futuristic McEwen-Adams blown Oldsmobile Shark car entry. McEwen had run as quick as 8.60 in the second round to defeat "Lefty" Mudersbach, but he slowed to a 9.08 in the final and had to settle for runner-up honors again when Nelson recorded an 8.71.

With the Detroit hot rods attracting larger numbers of fans each year with their intense brand rivalry, the battle for Stock supremacy between the many Chevy, Ford, Pontiac, Oldsmobile, Dodge, and Plymouth entries generated almost as much excitement as the Top Eliminator competition. The final was a true national showdown as Nicholson squared off against Strickler, whose Old Reliable Chevy was tuned by Bill "Grumpy" Jenkins; Nicholson won with a 12.84. Even more interest for the doorslammer contingent was created by the new Factory Experimental class that Hayden Proffitt won in Mickey Thompson's A/FX 434-cid Pontiac Tempest, which ran a 12.37 in the final to defeat the GET Special Dodge driven by Marvin Ford.

Other winners were Gary Cagle (Middle eliminator), Hugh Tucker (Little eliminator), "Bones" Balough (Junior eliminator), and Earl Wade (Street).

GARLITS DOMINATES AS TOP FUEL RETURNS

The return of the use of nitromethane to the Top Eliminator ranks was the big news at the third Winternationals. The move not only brought back such popular elements as engine cackle, header flames, and full-track tire-smoking runs but significant performance improvements as well. The previous event marks of 8.50, shared by Pete Robinson and Glen Ward, and 176.47 by Ward were shattered by Don Garlits (8.11) and the Weekly, Rivero, Fox & Holding entry (188.66 mph).

Garlits, who showed up with his wild Swamp Rat V entry, one of the first dragsters to successfully use an aerodynamic wing to provide downforce for extra traction on the top end, scored the first of his 35 Top

Fuel titles by defeating fellow Florida campaigner Art Malone in the final with times of 8.26 and 186.32.

The gas-burning rails, which had campaigned for Top Eliminator honors, now were grouped in the new Top Gas category. Many familiar drivers were competing, including 1961 Winternationals winner Jack Chrisman, 1962 champion Jim Nelson (with Danny Ongais now driving the Dragmaster Dart), Connie Kalitta, Gordon "Collecting" Collett, and Ward in a new Dodge-powered entry. The final pitted Kalitta's single-engine Chrysler against Peters & Frank's twin-small-block Chevy-powered Freight Train, which won with an 8.82, 178.21. John Peters was originally listed as the driver for the winning entry, but the car was actually piloted by Bob

Muravez, who used the fictitious name of Floyd Lippencott Jr. because his parents had forbidden him to race.

Detroit's Big Three were really in high gear with their concept of "Win on Sunday, sell on Monday." The Chevy and Ford Super Stock engines had expanded from their former respective sizes of 409 and 406 cid to 427, and the Dodge Plymouth entries had gone from 413 to 426. Other factory-developed performance enhancements included lightweight fiberglass or aluminum body panels, trunk-mounted batteries, and more refined multiple-carburetor induction systems.

The gains made by the Chrysler factory teams during the off-season paid off as they broke the two-year winning

streak of Don Nicholson's Chevrolets. With Stock entries limited to tire widths of 7 inches, the factory-backed Dodge and Plymouth entries took advantage of their Torque-flite automatic transmissions for more consistent launches off the starting line than their more traditional four-speed manual-transmission-equipped counterparts. Al Ekstrand scored in one of the team cars of the famed Ramchargers car club, which consisted of a group of elite Chrysler engineers who were also very talented racing enthusiasts. Ekstrand won with a 12.44, 115.08.

Other winners were Tony Nancy (Comp), Doug Cook (Middle eliminator), Richard Bourgeois (Little eliminator), and Hugh Tucker (Junior eliminator).

Don Garlits established himself as a successful innovator and scored his first of 35 Top Fuel titles. His Swamp Rat V had a traction-boosting wing on top of the engine.

Bob Muravez, who won Top Gas with John Peters' Freight Train, hid in the winner's circle because his parents had forbidden him to race. He used the alias Floyd Lippencott Jr.

(Above left) Al Ekstrand posted the first major NHRA win for the famed Ramchargers team with his Stock triumph. Ekstrand, a lawyer, would later field his own Lawman entries. (Above right) Renowned auto-upholstery specialist Tony Nancy won in Comp with his 22 Jr. entry, which featured a sleek roadster body designed by friend and artist Steve Swaja. (Right) Genuine Oldsmobile engines were very competitive in the early 1960s, as exemplified by the Olds-powered AA/GS Willys of Stone, Woods & Cook, which won Middle eliminator with Doug Cook driving.

1964

(Right) Jack Williams' relaxed appearance in the Top Fuel winner's circle belied his hectic journey to the final, which included a long drive on a snow-covered highway. (Below) Danny Ongais, near lane, defeated Mickey Thompson's Hemi Ford in the Top Gas final. Five years later, Ongais would drive Thompson's all-conquering Mustang Funny Car.

The increased interest of Detroit's Big Three in drag racing was exemplified by the debut of the Ford 427 Thunderbolts. Gas Ronda's entry, far lane, won S/S class honors.

Jeep Hampshire had quite a weekend in Top Fuel. He set low e.t. with a 7.85 and a new national record of 8.01, and he ran the second-fastest pass of the weekend, 195.22 mph.

In Sunday's Top Stock eliminations, the Mopars outlasted the Thunderbolts, and Tommy Grove's Plymouth, near lane, won in the heated factory contest.

WILLIAMS' FRANTIC THRASH PAYS OFF

When the Top Fuel champion was determined by pitting the winner of Saturday's class runoffs against the victor of Sunday's regular eliminations, the Saturday winner had many hours of sweating it out Sunday before getting a shot at the title. But Jack Williams, the 1964 Saturday winner, had plenty to keep him busy.

Williams had blown the only engine owned by the Williams & Swan team on his winning run Saturday afternoon, and after traveling back to his hometown of Bakersfield, Calif., and working late into the night to repair the powerplant, a raging snowstorm forced highway officials to close the old Highway 99 Ridge Route Sunday. But resourceful Williams not only talked his way into driving on the slippery road but also received a police escort. Williams reached Pomona in time for one checkout pass, then defeated Sunday's eliminations winner, "T.V. Tommy" Ivo, 8.16 to 8.24.

In Top Gas, Danny Ongais rebounded from losing Saturday's class final to Mickey Thompson's experimental Hemi-Ford-powered entry to take the overall honors Sunday. Ongais earned the right to meet Thompson for the title when he defeated defending Winternationals champion John Peters' Freight Train in the final of Sunday's Low Eight eliminations, 8.41 to 8.66. Thompson had made checkout runs of

8.74 and 8.56, and he was no match for Ongais in the trophy dash, in which the young Hawaiian driver took an 8.39 to 8.53 victory.

Rivaling the two dragster categories for spectator excitement was Top Stock eliminations, which featured many highly efficient factory-backed Dodge and Plymouth entries against Ford's wild new Thunderbolts, midsize Fairlanes with 427-cid engines shoehorned into the engine compartments. Gas Ronda had won S/S class honors with his Thunderbolt earlier in the weekend, and Jim Rodgers' Dodge had claimed the S/SA class title. But in Sunday's eliminations, the consistency of the automatic-transmission-equipped Mopars was too much for the Ford stick-shift entries, and Tommy Grove won Sunday's all-Plymouth final by driving to an 11.63 after Doug Lovegrove red-lighted.

The growing appeal of doorslammers prompted NHRA to add another major category, Factory Stock, which the new 427-cid Mercury Comets dominated. Don Nicholson set the pace with his one-of-a-kind station wagon, built to take advantage of the weight of the extra glass mounted above the rear tires for added traction, but Ronnie Sox's quicker starting-line reflexes defeated him in the final, 11.49 to 11.47.

Ron Root earned the Street title in his '63 Dart with a 14.24, and Charlie Smith scored Comp honors.

'SNAKE' WINS THE ONE-DAY WONDER

If an example of NHRA's organizational capabilities is ever needed, look to the 1965 Winternationals, at which heavy fog Friday and rain Saturday forced the event to be run entirely Sunday.

At the "Great One-Day Race," class eliminations, qualifying, and competition in seven eliminators were squeezed into a 10-hour window. A total of 3,168 runs were recorded, a feat that would not have been possible without the unwavering support and cooperation of the racers and excellent coordination by the NHRA staff, which Event Director Jack Hart oversaw.

Each of the day's seven victors was a first-time national event winner. Don "the Snake" Prudhomme led the way with a Top Fuel victory in his first major outing in Roland Leong's beautiful new Hawaiian entry. To earn his win, Prudhomme outlasted the challenges of Art Malone, who set low e.t. of the meet with a 7.56 blast, and Don Garlits, who established top speed at 206.88 mph. The field also included factory participation from Detroit: Chrysler's Ramchargers campaigned an entry with the relatively new late-model Hemi, and Connie Kalitta's Bounty Hunter had one of Ford's new SOHC 427 Hemi engines.

Prudhomme reached the final handily after wins against the teams of Carroll Bros. & Oxman, James Warren, Danny Ongais, and Rick Stewart. In the money round, "the Snake" defeated Bill Alexander with a

7.76 for the first of his 49 NHRA victories.

One of the more popular wins was Jimmy Nix's triumph in Top Gas, highlighted by an 8.55 to 8.74 conquest of Harrell Amyx in the final. Bill "Grumpy" Jenkins, who had earned fame as the tuner for Dave Strickler, showed he could drive too when he won Stock on a series of holeshots with his Black Arrow '65 Plymouth.

But the major focus for the factory hot rods was in Factory Stock, where Ford unveiled its new SOHC 427 Hemi-powered Mustang entries. They were slated to race radical altered-wheelbase Dodge and Plymouth vehicles, but they were deemed by NHRA not to be "factory stock," and the Chrysler contingent was forced to compete with four hastily prepared "legal" A/FX entries. The Fords won in overwhelming fashion; Bill Lawton's Tasca Ford Mustang took a 10.92 decision against Len Richter's Mustang in the final. Other big winners from the one-day spectacular were Chico Breschini (Comp), Ernie Dutre in the Dutre & Dutre entry (Street), and Dave Kempton (Junior Stock).

The combination of excessive fog Friday and rain all day Saturday forced the event to be run in its entirety Sunday.

Don "the Snake" Prudhomme scored his first national event Top Fuel victory with a flawless performance behind the wheel of Roland Leong's new Hawaiian.

Connie Kalitta, near lane, showed up with the first Top Fueler equipped with Ford's new 427-cid SOHC Hemi, and Art Malone set low e.t. of the meet at 7.56.

Ford entries dominated Factory Stock for the second year in a row. Bill Lawton's new SOHC 427-cid Hemi-powered Mustang defeated Roger Lindamood on the way to the title.

Chrysler's altered-wheelbase entries, which inspired the Funny Car moniker, were declared illegal for Factory Stock, but Butch Leal gave a hint of things to come with this exhibition run.

1966

SHAHAN IS SPORT'S FIRST FEMALE WINNER

No form of motorsports has enjoyed more success by female drivers than NHRA Drag Racing. Shirley Muldowney and Angelle Sampey have each won three world championships, and more than 10 women have scored Pro eliminator national event victories. Leading the way was Shirley Shahan, whose Top Stock win ended the days of the winner's circle being a male-only domain.

Because of the heated competition between Detroit brands for doorslammer supremacy, Top Stock always featured some of the best drivers in drag racing. Among those whom Shahan outlasted were 1964 Nationals winner

Roger Lindamood, 1964 Nationals S/S class winner Butch Leal, 1964 Junior Stock world champion Mike Schmitt, 1965 Winternationals Stock winner Bill "Grumpy" Jenkins, and future star Don Grotheer.

Driving the Drag-On-Lady S/SA '65 Plymouth tuned by her husband at the time, H.L., Shahan reached the final by defeating Schmitt, then won the title by overcoming the handicap head-start lead of Ken Heinemann's A/SA '66 Plymouth for the historic 11.26 triumph.

Competing for the attention generated by Shahan's monumental achievement was Mike Snively's Top Fuel victory in Roland Leong's Hawaiian.

Snively had big shoes to fill when he accepted the ride from Leong after Don "the Snake" Prudhomme decided to run his own team in 1966; he had won both major 1965 NHRA national events, the Winternationals and Nationals, with Leong's car.

The usual format of Saturday's AA/F class winner racing the victor of Sunday's eliminations was dispensed with after fog problems Saturday forced officials to drop class eliminations and expand Sunday's field to 32 cars. Snively was more than up to the task and capped his day with a classic 7.54 to 7.59 victory against Jim Dunn in the final. Like Prudhomme the year before, Snively would go on to score in

the same season at the Nationals with Leong's Hawaiian.

Though they didn't yet have an eliminator of their own, the Funny Cars that had burst on the scene with sudden popularity in 1965 were out in full force, competing in such classes as C/Fuel for the injected entries and CC/Fuel for those equipped with superchargers.

Other big winners were Gordon "Collecting" Collett in Top Gas, Hugh Tucker in Super (his third Winternationals victory), Jerry Harvey in Street (driving his A/FX Mustang to defeat Schmitt's B/FX Ford), Arnold Chaves in Comp with his D/A roadster, and local racer Wiley Cossey in Junior Stock.

Shirley Shahan beamed in the winner's circle after she became the first woman to win an eliminator title at a major NHRA national event with her victory in Top Stock.

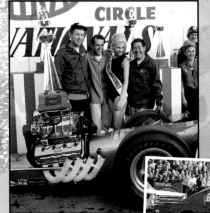

(Left) New driver Mike Snively proved equally capable in the cockpit of Roland Leong's Hawaiian as he repeated Don Prudhomme's 1965 Top Fuel win. (Below) Funny Cars, which had exploded in popularity in 1965, returned in 1966 but didn't yet have a category of their own. Gas Ronda won the C/Fuel class with his Mustang.

(Right) Gordon Collett, near lane, scored the first of his three Winternationals Top Gas wins by defeating Tommy Larkin in the final with an 8.33, 189.86. (Far right) Local favorite Wiley Cossey drove his big-block Chevy-powered B/S entry to an impressive victory in Junior Stock against Robert Chisea in the final.

KALITTA'S FORD LEADS WAY WITH 7.17

After helping Ford develop its 427-cid SOHC Hemi for Top Fuel racing for three years, Connie Kalitta finally saw his efforts pay off big time with a dominating win. The Fords had produced race-winning horsepower from the beginning, but at times, they lacked the strength to survive five rounds of grueling eliminations in the 32-car fields. It was apparent that Kalitta and the Ford engineers had solved that problem when he drove his Bounty Hunter entry to times of 7.28, 7.24, 7.22, and 7.23 to reach the final, where he upped the nitro percentage a bit to unleash a 7.17, low e.t. of the meet, to dispose of Gene Goleman.

Before his loss to Kalitta, Goleman was having a career weekend with runs as quick as 7.27 and wins against Leroy Goldstein, Dave Beebe, and Danny Ongais.

Gordon "Collecting" Collett became the first driver to win two consecutive Top Gas titles at the Winternationals when he defeated future Top Fuel star Kelly Brown, 8.09 to 8.15.

Super eliminator proved to be a real crowd-pleaser with a wide variety of exciting entries, ranging from "Wild Willie" Borsch's Winged Express AA/Fuel Altered to Funny Cars that included Don Nicholson's Eliminator I Mercury Comet, which had won the S/XS category, and Gene Snow's Rambunctious Dodge, winner of the C/FD class. But in the end, the Kohler Bros.' more conventional supercharged big-block Chevy-powered A/GS Anglia, driven by Ed Kohler, won the title by defeating the famed roadster of three-time Winternationals winner Hugh Tucker.

The big news in the doorslammer ranks was the introduction of the new multi-class Super Stock format. Once reserved for only the fastest Detroit machines that raced on a heads-up basis, Super Stock was opened to the increasing number of muscle cars that baby boomers were buying and racing. The Ford and Mopar factory-backed teams worked overtime in the off-season to prepare for this race, as did the large contingent of so-called independent Chevrolet racers such as Bill "Grumpy" Jenkins. However, previously unheralded Eddie Vasquez scored a huge upset win with his SS/C Chevy II by outlasting a field that included Jenkins, Sox & Martin, Shirley Shahan, Arlen Vanke, Dave Kempton, Ed Miller, and many others.

Also reaching the winner's circle were Chico Breschini (Comp), Richard Wood (Street), and Graham Douglas (Stock).

Connie Kalitta ran a string of 7.2s before uncorking a 7.17, low e.t. of the meet, in the Top Fuel final to defeat Gene Goleman.

Conspicuous by his absence in the Top Fuel field was Don "Big Daddy" Garlits, who also failed to make the Springnationals show before rebounding with a huge win in Indy. (Below) The factory teams were out in full force for the first running of NHRA's expanded Super Stock program, but they were sidelined by independent Eddie Vasquez.

(Left) "Cheating Chico" Breschini, who acquired his nickname simply because he won so much, repeated his 1965 Comp victory with his Chevy-powered B/D.

The popular Kohler Bros. big-block Chevy-powered AA/Gas Supercharged Anglia, driven by Ed Kohler, won from a wild Super eliminator field.

James Warren drove the Warren-Coburn-Miller Top Fueler to victory at the 1968 Winternationals. He made a single run for the title when Dwight Salisbury was a no-show.

Ford's Cobra Jet Mustangs made a successful debut. Driving one of the eight SS/E entries, Al Joniec, far lane, defeated Dave Wren's Mopar in the Super Stock final.

(Above) Gene Snow, the 1967 Nationals Super eliminator victor, switched from fuel to gas and scored in Comp with his Rambunctious Dart. (Below) Gordon Collett qualified last and finished first in Top Gas, defeating Jack Jones in the final for his third straight Winternationals title.

Don "the Snake" Prudhomme teamed with Cobra creator Carroll Shelby and debuted his Ford Cammer-powered Top Fueler, Shelby's Super Snake, which won the Best Engineered award.

WARREN TERRORIZES; FORD'S COBRA JET DEBUTS

Known as the Ridge Route Terrors, for the historic highway that linked early Los Angeles with California's central valley, Bakersfield's James Warren and longtime partner Roger Coburn lived up to their nickname with a clear victory in Top Fuel. Not only was the Warren-Coburn-Miller dragster the quickest and fastest of the 84 entries, but it also was the first time at a major NHRA event that the Top Fuel champion made a single for the title. And Warren did it without smoking the tires, leaving his car in plain view from start to finish.

Warren served notice that he was the one to beat in round one, setting low e.t. and top speed with a sizzling 6.87, 230.76 against Jerry Ruth. After stopping Bob Downey with a 7.08 in round two, Warren squared off against the man who had defeated him for the Nationals title a year earlier with a final-round holeshot, "Big Daddy" Don Garlits. Warren got the better of Garlits this time, 7.03 to 7.25, then stopped Dave Beebe in the semifinals, 7.26 to 7.29. Unfortunately for runner-up Dwight Salisbury, the final was lost in the pits, where he and his crew couldn't replace a worn-out clutch in time to compete for the title.

Ford's Cobra Jet Mustangs also made headlines with their debuts in Super Stock.

Uniform in appearance and equipped with Ford's new 428-cid Cobra Jet engine, the eight SS/E entries were driven by a who's who of the era's top drivers, namely "Dyno Don" Nicholson, Gas Ronda, Al Joniec, Hubert Platt, Jerry Harvey, Carl Holbrook, Bill Ireland, and Phil Bonner. It was a successful debut, to be sure. Joniec beat Platt for class honors and defeated Dave Wren's Mopar in the Super Stock final.

Teaming with Cobra creator Carroll Shelby, Don "the Snake" Prudhomme debuted his Ford Cammer-powered Top Fueler, Shelby's Super Snake. Prudhomme lost to Salisbury on a holeshot in the quarterfinals, but the car was voted Best Engineered.

Gordon Collett qualified last and finished first to collect his third straight Winternationals Top Gas title, and unheralded Rich Galli drove his A/FD to victory in Super eliminator after making the field as an alternate. Gene Snow, winner of the 1967 Nationals in Super eliminator, switched from fuel to gas and took the Comp title with his familiar Rambunctious Dart, and Bo Laws and John Barkley won Street and Stock, respectively.

"Wild Willie" Borsch wheeled the famed Marcellus & Borsch fuel altered to an AA/FA record of 7.29 in Super eliminator qualifying, then lost in round one when his unpredictable machine made a typical guardrail-to-centerline, tire-spinning run.

MULLIGAN TOPS LIST OF FIRST-TIMERS

After a string of six big-meet runner-ups in the previous two years, including at the Springnationals and World Finals in 1968, John "the Zoo Keeper" Mulligan drove Tim Beebe's green-striped Beebe & Mulligan dragster to the team's only NHRA Top Fuel victory at the 1969 Winternationals. Mulligan wasn't the only first-time winner. In fact, all eight of the event champions had never won a major NHRA event.

Mulligan's victory was as impressive as it was popular. Just qualifying for the 32-car field proved difficult, as evidenced by the list of those who didn't. Relegated to the role of spectator on Sunday were some of the most celebrated names in the sport,

including Don Garlits, Tommy Ivo, Tom McEwen, Mike Snively, John Wiebe, and Marvin Schwartz. Larry Dixon Sr. set the pace with a track record 6.81, and four drivers, including Mulligan, tied for top-speed honors at 225.00 mph.

After a 7.12 in his first-round win against Tom Larkin, Mulligan displayed the kind of six-second performance that had made him a quarter-mile star, running 6.85, 6.86, and 6.93 in respective victories against defending Winter-nationals champion James Warren, reigning world champion Bennie Osborn, and Leroy Goldstein. In the final, Mulligan ran a 6.95 to easily defeat Don Prudhomme, who, after suffering engine damage in his semifinal victory against

Jim Dunn, slowed to an 8.52.

At the Nationals later that year, Mulligan rocked the sport with a 6.43 that was more than two-tenths of a second quicker than the NHRA national record. Sadly, Mulligan was badly burned in a first-round accident at that event and died weeks later.

In Funny Car, Clare Sanders drove "Jungle Jim" Liberman's Chevy II to his only NHRA national event title with a final-round victory against Ray Alley. After easy defeats of Kelly Chadwick and Ron Leslie, Sanders set low e.t. of eliminations with a 7.80 in an even easier semifinal victory against Leonard Hughes, who coasted to an 11.30 after his engine let go. Like the others, Alley proved no match for

Sanders in the final. Despite his best effort of the weekend, an 8.11, Alley finished a distant second to Sanders' 7.88.

After enjoying considerable success with his series of Hawaiian dragsters, Roland Leong debuted his first Funny Car in spectacular fashion. With Larry Reyes behind the wheel, Leong's brand-new Charger got loose and took flight just past the finish line in a first-round win against Mike Hamby. Reyes was not injured, but the car was destroyed.

Rounding out the list of first-time major NHRA event winners were Don Grotheer (Super Stock), Dave Grassi (Top Gas), Ken Dondero (Super eliminator), Ed Sigmon (Comp), Dick Landy (Street), and Mark Coletti (Stock).

Roland Leong's first Hawaiian Funny Car made a memorable debut. The Larry Reyes-driven Charger took flight just past the finish line in a first-round win against Mike Hamby.

(Above left) John Mulligan, left, and car owner and engine builder Tim Beebe teamed for their only NHRA Top Fuel victory at the 1969 Winternationals. (Above right) All eight of the 1969 champions had never won a major NHRA event, including Clare Sanders, who drove "Jungle Jim" Liberman's Chevy II to an impressive Funny Car victory.

(Far right) Runner-up to Ronnie Sox at the 1968 Springnationals, Don Grotheer drove his SS/BA '68 Barracuda to the win in Super Stock. (Right) Dave Grassi took Top Gas honors with 7.71 to 7.61 holeshot victory against Cliff Smith in the final.

Driving the same big-block-powered '68 Camaro that he raced in Super Stock, Bill "Grumpy" Jenkins defeated Ronnie Sox's legendary '70 Barracuda in the final to take NHRA's first Pro Stock event title.

(Right) Roland Leong, second from right, and driver Larry Reyes accepted the Funny Car trophy from Car Craft magazine's John Raffa. (Below) Larry Dixon Sr. wheeled his Howard Cam Rattler to victory in Top Fuel.

Jack Ditmars drove his fan-favorite Buick Opel, running as an A/Fuel Altered, to a popular win in Comp.

Barrie Poole became the first Canadian to win a major NHRA event when he drove his SS/H Mustang to victory in Super Stock.

JENKINS WINS INAUGURAL PRO STOCK EVENT

The 1970 Winternationals was a significant event for a couple of reasons because not only did it feature separate groups for the Professional and Sportsman categories for the first time, but it also introduced a new category: Pro Stock. Driving the same big-block-powered '68 Camaro that he previously raced in Super Stock, Bill "Grumpy" Jenkins defeated Ronnie Sox's legendary '70 Barracuda in the final round to take NHRA's first Pro Stock event title.

After qualifying No. 2 with a 10.08 behind Sox's 10.00, Jenkins was the only driver to dip into the nines, wheeling his Grumpy's Toy IV to three sub-10-second runs in eliminations. He sandwiched a pair of 9.98s around an early shutoff 10.26 in respective victories over Bill Hielscher, Mike Fons, and a red-lighting Dick Landy. In the final, Jenkins left first and never looked back, running a 9.99 at 139.53 mph (top speed of the meet) against Sox's 10.12.

Larry Dixon Sr. won the Top Fuel title with a 6.80 to 7.48 final-round victory over sentimental favorite Tony Nancy. Driving his new Howard Cam Rattler, Dixon qualified No. 3 (6.78) in a 32-car Top Fuel field that included 19 six-second cars. He ran a 6.86 to beat Jim Paoli in round one and soloed to an easy 8.45 in round two when James Warren was a no-show. Dixon duplicated his qualifying time in the quarterfinals to turn back Ronnie Hampshire, but he

used up his engine in the process. With help from Hampshire's crew, Dixon swapped engines and made it back in time for his semifinal tussle with Tommy Ivo, who red-lighted.

Larry Reyes and Roland Leong bounced back from their spectacular first-round aerial act at the 1969 Winternationals by outlasting a star-studded Funny Car field. After squeezing into the 16-car field with a 7.73, Reyes ran a 7.54 in round one to beat Rich Siroonian and advanced to the final on red-lights by Kelly Chadwick and Leonard Hughes. After setting low e.t. with a 7.30 in his semifinal victory over Ken Stafford, Gene Snow appeared to have the upper hand going into the final, but Reyes jumped out to an early lead and held on with a 7.67 against Snow's slowing 7.83.

Don Hampton won the Top Gas title when a heavily favored Bob Muravez, driving John Peters' famous Freight Train, red-lighted in the final. Jack Ditmars drove his fan-favorite Buick Opel, running as an A/Fuel Altered, to a popular win in Comp, defeating 1969 Winternationals Super eliminator champion Ken Dondero. Dick Landy won his second straight Winternationals title, this time in Modified eliminator, Barrie Poole became the first Canadian to win a major NHRA event when he drove his Sandy Elliot-sponsored Mustang to victory in Super Stock, and Richard Charbonneau claimed top honors in Stock.

GARLITS WINS WITH INNOVATIVE DRAGSTER

Don Garlits proved that his rear-engine Top Fuel dragster was not only safer but also competitive when he made the supposedly unworkable design a winner in its NHRA national event debut at the 1971 Winternationals.

Garlits, running without the rear wing he would later add, qualified No. 9 in the 32-car field with a 6.80. He then got progressively quicker in each round up to the final, running low e.t. in three of the five rounds. Garlits defeated Tommy Allen, 6.85 to 6.89; John Nichols, 6.72 to 6.85; Carl Olson, 6.72 to 10.61; Jim Dunn, 6.70 to 7.58; and, in the final, spun the tires to an uncontested sixth NHRA national event victory at 7.03 over a broken Kenny Safford. Henry Harrison ran both low e.t. and top speed of the event, 6.61 and 223.32 mph, driving the Ewell, Bell & Goodwin dragster.

Sadly, at the same event where Garlits was helping make Top Fuel safer, 1961 Nationals Top Eliminator winner and innovator "Sneaky Pete" Robinson was killed on Saturday when his Top Fueler crashed on a 6.77-second qualifying run.

Roland Leong won Funny Car for the second straight year with his Hawaiian entry and Butch Maas behind the wheel. The No. 4 qualifier with a 7.12, Maas ran a 7.16 in an easy first-round win over Kenny Goodell and defeated a wheelstanding Rich Siroonian after smoking the tires in a wild quarterfinal race. After

making a single run in the semifinals when his scheduled opponent, Gene Snow, was a no-show, Maas won the final convincingly over Leroy Goldstein, setting low e.t. and top speed of the meet with a 6.93 at 212.76 mph. Goldstein, driving the Ramchargers entry, trailed with a 7.08, his best run of the event.

After losing to Bill Jenkins in the first NHRA Pro Stock final a year earlier, Ronnie Sox scored a seemingly effortless victory in the factory hot rod category. The slick-shifting half of the famed Sox & Martin team paced the 32-car field with an unreal 9.81 and ran 9.90, 9.82, 9.89, 9.85, and 9.86 in resepective victories over Richard Mirarcki, Bob Lambeck, Jenkins, Arlen Vanke, and Wally Booth.

Garlits' car wasn't the only unique winning dragster at the event. Walt Stevens, driving Ken Theiss' Odd Couple Top Gas dragster, won that eliminator in its last year of existence with a small-block Chevy and a Hemi engine mounted in tandem. Driving another notable car of the period, Don Enriquez won Comp with Gene Adams' early Hemi-powered injected-nitro A/FD, and Barrie Poole, whose win at the 1970 Winternationals made him the first Canadian to win a major NHRA event, won again in Super Stock. Reigning world champion Carroll Caudle won Modified eliminator, and Dave Boertman won Stock.

Don Garlits proved that his rear-engine Top Fuel dragster was not only safer but also competitive, making the supposedly unworkable design a winner in its NHRA national event debut.

Butch Maas drove Roland Leong's Hawaiian entry to the Funny Car title, which was the second straight win for Leong at the event.

After losing to Bill Jenkins in the first NHRA Pro Stock final a year earlier, Ronnie Sox collected his 10th major NHRA event trophy and fifth in Pro Stock.

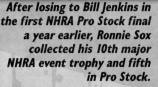

Walt Stevens, driving Ken Theiss' Odd Couple dragster, won Top Gas in its last year of existence with a small-block Chevy and a Hemi engine mounted in tandem.

Don Enriquez won Comp with Gene Adams' early Hemi-powered injected-nitro A/FD.

JENKINS RETURNS TO TOP OF PRO STOCK

Taking advantage of NHRA's new Pro Stock weight breaks, Bill "Grumpy" Jenkins drove his new small-block Chevy-powered Vega to a stunning victory at the 1972 Winternationals. Concerned that the overwhelming success of the Chrysler Hemi cars during the class' first two years could hurt the class, NHRA implemented separate weight breaks for small- and big-block entries for 1972, a move that would help Jenkins win six of the eight races that year and the NHRA Pro Stock championship.

Tuning problems held Jenkins to a qualifying best of 9.90, which put him in the 17th position of the 32-car field and forced him to race Stu McDade, driver of Billy Stepp's Challenger, which had qualified

No. 1 with a 9.59. But Jenkins made suspension changes prior to the first round and ran a 9.62 to defeat McDade's 9.75. Jenkins went on to defeat four more Hemi cars — Bill Bagshaw's Challenger, Melvin Yow's Challenger, Don Carlton's Barracuda, and Don Grotheer's Barracuda — en route to a crowd-pleasing victory. As he had done all day, Jenkins left first in the final and ran a 9.68 against Grotheer's 9.82 for his first win in nearly two years.

Jenkins wasn't the only upset winner at the 1972 event. After qualifying an inconspicuous 29th in the 32-car Top Fuel field with a 6.87, Carl Olson drove partner Mike Kuhl's dragster to a succession of 6.6-second runs en route to

his first NHRA national event title. Olson set the tone for this surprising victory with back-to-back 6.60s to stop Chris Karamesines and Tony Nancy. In his closest race of the day, Olson ran a 6.63 to defeat Dwight Salisbury's 6.70 in the quarterfinals and then made a single run in the semi's when his opponent, Gary Cochran, was forced to shut off with a fuel leak. Having run consistent 6.5s and top speed of the meet (231.95 mph), Olson's final-round opponent, Dennis Baca, appeared to have the advantage, but he smoked the tires, giving Olson an easy win.

Ed McCulloch and partner Ed Whipple debuted their Revellution Duster with a win in Funny Car. After running a sixth-best 6.93 in qualifying,

McCulloch defeated Jerry Ruth in a close first-round race, 6.90 to 6.96, then thundered to a track record 6.65 to beat defending event champion Butch Maas. After an easy semifinal win over a red-lighting Jake Johnston, McCulloch backed up his earlier 6.65 with a 6.68 to defeat Dale Pulde in rematch of their 1971 U.S. Nationals final that McCulloch also won.

Steve Woods drove his BB/Gas Supercharged Anglia to victory in Comp, and Fred Teixeira won Modified eliminator with his family's B/Gas Corvette. After an off-season restructuring of both classes, Judy Lilly became the third woman to win an NHRA national event title with her victory in Super Stock, and David Benisek won Stock.

Ed McCulloch and partner Ed Whipple debuted their Revellution Duster with a win in Funny Car, defeating Dale Pulde in a repeat of the 1971 U.S. Nationals final.

Upsets by Bill "Grumpy" Jenkins, who drove his new small-block Chevy-powered Vega (above left) to a stunning victory in Pro Stock, and Top Fuel winner Carl Olson (above right) highlighted the 1972 event.

(Far right) Judy Lilly became the third woman to win an NHRA national event title with her victory in Super Stock. (Right) NHRA Executive Vice President Jack Hart presented the Best Engineered Car award to Jim Dunn for his Woody Gilmore-built rear-engine Funny Car.

GARLITS WINS AGAIN

After a two-week postponement due to rain, the 1973 Winternationals delivered Professional titles to a trio of veterans. Top Fuel's winningest driver, "Big Daddy" Don Garlits, who won his first NHRA Top Fuel title at this event a decade previous, scored his third Winternationals victory and ninth overall. First-time Winternationals winner Don Schumacher moved into a tie with Ed McCulloch for the most Funny Car victories (five), and "Dyno Don" Nicholson, who first gained notice with his Super Stock win at the inaugural Winternationals in 1961, won his fifth national event title and second in Pro Stock.

Hampered by adverse track conditions, Garlits called on his experience to coax the best performance from his new Wynn's Charger Dodge-powered Top Fueler, setting both e.t. and top speed. After running a 6.60 in a decisive first-round win over Herm Petersen, Garlits unloaded the quickest run of the event, a 6.51, in round two against Terry Capp. Denver Schutz's red-light advanced Garlits to the semi's, where he easily outran Jack Martin, 6.54 to 6.83. He then beat an up-in-smoke Dennis Baca in the final with a 235.60-mph blast, the fastest run of the event, relegating Baca to his second straight Winternationals runner-up.

Like Garlits, Funny Car winner Schumacher was the quickest and fastest in his class. Schumacher guided his Stardust 'Cuda to a 7.64 in an easy first-round win over a tire-smoking Ron O'Donnell, then ran 7.43 and 7.26 in respective victories over Tom Hoover and Jim Murphy before dropping the hammer in the final with a 7.18 at 220.58 mph (low e.t. and top speed) against upstart Kenny Bernstein. Driving Ray Alley's Charger, Bernstein held a slight lead over Schumacher when his blower belt let go.

Nicholson, who won Winternationals Super Stock titles in 1961 and 1962, was by far the most consistent in Pro Stock. After qualifying his Lenco-equipped, small-block Ford-powered Pinto with a 9.38, Nicholson turned in low e.t. of the first round with a 9.45, besting Larry Breaux. He beat Butch Leal in round two with a 9.55, his slowest run of eliminations, and then with a bye into the final on the line, ran another 9.45 to defeat Dick Landy in the quarterfinals. Saving his best for last, Nicholson won the final with a 9.33 over No. 1 qualifier Don Carlton's off-pace 9.64. Nicholson's 9.33 gave him the NHRA national record, eclipsing the 9.34 that Carlton had run in the semifinals an hour earlier.

Steve Woods won his second straight Winternationals title in Comp, and Bob Riffle won Modified eliminator with his all-conquering Rod Shop Dodge. Paul Smith won Super Stock over defending event champion Judy Lilly, and Les Young won Stock.

A decade after winning his first NHRA Top Fuel title at this event, Don Garlits drove his new Wynn's Charger Dodge-powered dragster to his third Winternationals victory.

Don Schumacher guided his Stardust Barracuda, near lane, to a final-round victory over Kenny Bernstein in Funny Car. Bernstein, driving Ray Alley's Charger, held a slight lead when his blower belt let go.

(Left) "Dyno Don" Nicholson's small-block Ford-powered Pinto was the class of the field in Pro Stock. In the final, Nicholson defeated No. 1 qualifier Don Carlton's Mopar Missile (below) with a national record 9.33, eclipsing the 9.34 that Carlton had run in the semifinals an hour earlier.

Steve Woods drove his BB/Gas Supercharged Anglia to his second straight Winternationals title in Comp.

1974

(Above) After losing the final and Top Fuel world championship to Jerry Ruth at the World Finals in October, Gary Beck turned the tables on Ruth in the final at the 1974 season opener. (Right) NHRA President and founder Wally Parks presented the Funny Car trophy to Dale Emery, who won in his first race following a spectacular crash at the Supernationals in November.

Bill "Grumpy" Jenkins retired his Grumpy's Toy X Vega in style with his fourth Winternationals victory and 10th of his Pro Stock career.

Dale Armstrong won NHRA's newest category, Pro Comp, over Ken Veney in a classic confrontation between Armstrong's A/Fuel Dragster and Veney's BB/Funny Car.

Les Young drove his U/SA Chevy wagon to his second straight Winternationals victory in Stock.

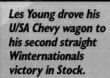

BECK RIDES ROUGHSHOD OVER FIELD

In what was a virtual carbon copy of his stunning performance that earned him his second U.S. Nationals title in 1973, Gary Beck drove Ray Peets' recently revamped and still-unpainted dragster to an impressive Top Fuel victory. Beck used a barrage of five-second runs to overwhelm the quickest field in Winternationals history, which included reigning world champion Jerry Ruth. Not to be outdone, Dale Emery outlasted the event's quickest Funny Car field, driving Jeg Coughlin's rebuilt Camaro, which had been badly damaged in a crash three months earlier. Emery made a single run in the final after reigning world champion Frank Hall broke. Bill "Grumpy" Jenkins became the all-time leader in Winternationals victories with four when he defeated reigning world champion Wayne Gapp in the Pro Stock final.

Beck, who would go on to win the Springnationals and Le Grandnational en route to his first of two world titles under NHRA's new championship points system, qualified No. 4 with a 6.02 and ran 5.96, 5.90, 5.84 (low e.t. of the meet), and 5.94 at 243.24 mph (top speed) in respective victories over John Austin, John Wiebe, Pat Dakin, and Ruth for his only Winternationals win. Beck's victory over Ruth was especially gratifying because he lost the final and the world championship to Ruth at the World Finals in October.

Emery's Funny Car victory was made all the more impressive by the fact that it came in his first race following a spectacular crash in his semifinal win at the Supernationals in November. After extensive repairs to the car — the chassis was rebuilt and fitted with a swoopy new '74 body — Emery ran a 6.47 on his only qualifying pass and 6.38, 6.46, and 6.47 in respective wins over Don Prudhomme, Dale Pulde, and John Collins before making his best run of the weekend in the final, a 6.36.

Jenkins retired his Grumpy's Toy X Vega in style with his 10th Pro Stock victory and what had to be one of his toughest. After defeating fellow Chevy racer Paul Blevins in round one with a 9.05, all that stood between Jenkins and victory were three eight-second Fords. He dispatched the first two with relative ease, downing Melvin Yow, 8.94 to 9.12, and setting low e.t. by beating Bob Glidden, 8.91 to 9.09, but in the final, Jenkins took a slight early lead and held on for a narrow 8.93 to 8.94 victory against Gapp.

Dale Armstrong won NHRA's newest category, Pro Comp, which made its debut at the Supernationals, over Ken Veney in a classic confrontation between Armstrong's A/Fuel Dragster and Veney's BB/Funny Car. Les Young was a repeat winner in Stock, and Ron Bonfanti, Lee Shepherd, and Marcel Cloutier won Comp, Modified eliminator, and Super Stock, respectively.

'SNAKE' KICKS OFF HIS REIGN OF TERROR

Hometown hero Don "the Snake" Prudhomme kicked off the best two years of his legendary driving career by winning the Funny Car title at the 15th annual Winternationals, his second of five triumphs at the season opener and his first in 10 years, since his breakthrough win in Top Fuel at the 1965 event.

From behind the wheel of his vaunted U.S. Army-sponsored Chevy Monza, Prudhomme set the pace for a season in which he would win six of the eight events on the schedule and his first of four straight championships. He would win the Winternationals each of the next two years as well, using the 1976 win as a springboard to a seven-of-eight-win season.

Prudhomme qualified No. 2 with a dazzling 6.25 — second only to Bill Leavitt's surprising low e.t. blast of 6.21 — and closed with a better-yet 6.24 in the final to defeat Mike Miller in Jim Green's Green Elephant Vega; the runner-up was the second in a row for the Washington car owner.

Prudhomme was joined in the winner's circle by a pair of fellow future Hall of Famers, "Big Daddy" Don Garlits, who scored in Top Fuel, and Bob Glidden, who collected the win in Pro Stock.

For his fourth Winternationals win, Garlits had to come from well back in the field. He qualified just 12th (a stat that wasn't as bad as it sounds; the field was packed very tightly with just .16-second separating the 5.937 of surprise No. 1 qualifier Paul Longenecker and No. 16 Dick LaHaie's 6.098) and needed a little luck in round one, then called on his tuning wiles to do the rest.

Garlits' hopes of winning the event appeared to go up in smoke in round one when he lost traction against No. 4 qualifier Don Ewald, but Ewald had been lined up incorrectly by his crewmembers and crossed the centerline, giving Garlits new life. Garlits pounded out his best run of the meet, a 6.00, to dispatch LaHaie, then beat Rick Ramsey in the semifinals and tire-smoking Dave Settles in the Candies & Hughes dragster in the final for his 12th win.

Glidden scored in a retro-looking '70 Mustang, a replacement to his successful Pintos that took advantage of a new weight break afforded longer-wheelbase cars and gave him his first Winternationals crown and an 8.77 national record. Glidden posted his win, just the fifth of what would become a dominating 85-victory total, in a final-round decision against Wayne Gapp's similarly long-wheelbased four-door Maverick.

Pro Comp champ Don Enriquez won his second Winternationals Wally and was joined by fellow Sportsman winners Phil Featherston (Comp), David Andrews (Modified), John Lingenfelter (Super Stock), and Tom Tereau (Stock).

Don "the Snake" Prudhomme debuted his vaunted U.S. Army-sponsored Monza with a victory, then won five more times in 1975 en route to his first Funny Car world championship.

"Big Daddy" Don Garlits scored the fourth Winternationals Top Fuel victory of his legendary career. The wily Florida veteran captured his 12th win with a final-round victory against Dave Settles.

(Above) Bob Glidden, far lane, and Wayne Gapp were driving long-wheelbase Fords to take advantage of a new Pro Stock rule. Glidden's Mustang, far lane, defeated Gapp's four-door Maverick for the title. (Right) NHRA President Wally Parks congratulated Don Enriquez after his Pro Comp conquest. Enriquez had won the season opener four years earlier in Comp.

John Lingenfelter collected his first of two Winternationals Wallys in his SS/MA Corvette. The late, great engine builder would win again in Pomona in Comp two years later.

1976

Frank Bradley scored his first national event win in Top Fuel. "The Beard" won four NHRA Wallys, including two in Pomona, the second in 1991.

Don Prudhomme won seven of eight 1976 NHRA Funny Car titles, beginning in Pomona, where he scored his third Winternationals crown and tied Ronnie Sox as the sport's winningest driver.

As they had the previous year, Ford favorites Bob Glidden, near lane, and Wayne Gapp dueled in the Pro Stock final, which Glidden again won.

After a runner-up to teammate Dale Armstrong in 1974, Ken Veney, near lane, scored his first Winternationals Pro Comp victory, besting Jerry Darien in the final.

Phil Featherston won Comp for the second straight year with his popular supercharged Opel when he defeated future Super Gas world champ Mike Ferderer in the final.

'SNAKE,' GLIDDEN REPEAT; BRADLEY WINS FIRST

Don Prudhomme and Bob Glidden repeated their 1975 triumphs in Funny Car and Pro Stock, respectively, and were joined by upset Top Fuel winner Frank Bradley at the U.S. bicentennial-year edition of the Winternationals.

The win by Bradley, known to fans and fellow racers as "the Beard," was a cut above for the Napa, Calif., veteran racer: It was his first in national event competition. He collected the victory in a razor-close final-round battle with fellow California veteran James Warren and the vaunted Ridge Route Terrors entry. Warren was out of the gate first, but Bradley reeled him in, 5.93 to 6.01. Bradley would win four national events, two in Pomona, also winning there in 1991. Dale Funk set low e.t. with a 5.78 that led qualifying.

Prudhomme's Funny Car triumph, the second of three straight in Pomona for the newly crowned world champ, was historic in that it was his 15th win and tied him with Pro Stock's Ronnie Sox as the winningest driver in NHRA history. Prudhomme's win at the Gatornationals in Florida a month later would make him the sport's all-time-winningest driver, a rank he held for years before being surpassed by Glidden.

Prudhomme's win in his Army-sponsored Monza was his seventh in nine outings with the car, dating back to his win at the 1975 season opener, and Prudhomme would win seven of eight events on the 1976 calendar. Prudhomme, who just a few months earlier had shattered the six-second barrier with a 5.97 in nearby Ontario, Calif., during the 1975 World Finals, ran the second-quickest pass in class history, a 6.02, in qualifying and backed it up with a first-round 6.06 to set the national record. Following a massive pit thrash after burning five pistons and breaking the rear end in defeating Tom Prock, father of current nitro crew chief Jimmy Prock, in the semifinals, "the Snake" defeated 1972 Winternationals champ Ed "the Ace" McCulloch in the final.

For the second straight year, the Pro Stock title round pitted Glidden against fellow Ford campaigner Wayne Gapp, and for the second straight year, the win light shone in Glidden's lane. While Gapp was still piloting the four-door Maverick dubbed the Taxi by fans, two-time world champ Glidden was back behind the wheel of a familiar Pinto. Both battled through what then was the quickest Pro Stock field ever assembled to square off in the final, where Glidden won easily, 8.82 to 8.91.

Phil Featherston won Comp for the second straight year to lead all Sportsman champs, a roster that included hard-running Ken Veney (Pro Comp), local favorite Butch "the California Flash" Leal (Modified), Larry Tores (Super Stock), and Jerry McClanahan (Stock).

'KING' CROWNS FUELERS; IT'S 'SNAKE' AGAIN

Don Prudhomme won the Winternationals for a record-setting third straight time and the fourth overall and was joined in the winner's circle by a pair of first-time winners of the season opener, Jerry Ruth in Top Fuel and Larry Lombardo in Pro Stock.

Although Prudhomme had retired his trusty John Buttera-built Monza Funny Car (which racked up 13 wins in 16 events in 1975 and 1976) for a Pat Foster-fabricated Plymouth Arrow, there was no stopping "the Snake" again in Pomona. The two-time world champ added victory No. 22 to his résumé with another strong performance. In the final round, Prudhomme put down the challenge of Raymond Beadle, who had emerged as his greatest challenger the last two seasons and whose 1979 season title would ultimately end Prudhomme's string of world championships at four. On this occasion, though, "the Snake" shot down the driver of the Blue Max Mustang with a stout 6.03, the third-quickest official time in class history behind his own two five-second passes.

Ruth, the 1973 world champ — back when the winner of the annual NHRA World Finals was crowned the season champ — won his first race since that triumph and did it by upsetting four-time Winternationals champ Don Garlits in the final round, 5.99 to 6.38. Garlits to that point in his career already had established an unearthly final-round win record of 15-5 (60 percent), including victories in his six most recent final-round appearances. Ruth, the vaunted "King of the Northwest," was hot off of his runner-up at the 1976 World Finals and parlayed that momentum into a big win, his second of three career victories.

Lombardo had ended Bob Glidden's two-season Pro Stock world championship streak in 1976, then ended his two-year Winternationals dominance to kick off his title defense. At the wheel of four-time Winternationals champ Bill "Grumpy" Jenkins' Grumpy's Toy Chevy Monza, Lombardo, who took over the wheel from Jenkins at the 1976 Gatornationals, won the Winternationals in his first Pro appearance at the event by stopping Ford veteran "Dyno Don" Nicholson and his Mustang II in the final, 8.61 to 8.77.

Prudhomme was not the lone repeat winner as John Lingenfelter, the 1975 winner in Super Stock, won his second Winternationals crown, this time in Comp, and Dave Boertman, who won the Stock title at the 1971 event, returned to the winner's circle by bagging the Super Stock victory. Dave Settles, the runner-up in Top Fuel at the 1975 Winternationals, won in Pro Comp, and future Pro Stock racer Tony Christian scored in Modified and Chad Langdon in Stock.

Don Prudhomme's U.S. Army Arrow debuted with a victory in Pomona, Prudhomme's 14th victory in the last 17 races. He defeated Raymond Beadle in the Funny Car final.

(Above) Jerry Ruth, near lane, upset "Big Daddy" Don Garlits in the Top Fuel title round for his second of three career wins. Garlits had won in his previous six final rounds. (Left) NHRA President Wally Parks, center, congratulated driver Larry Lombardo, right, the reigning world champ, and team owner Bill "Grumpy" Jenkins on their Pro Stock victory.

John Lingenfelter drove his A/Econo Altered Monza Comp entry to his second Winternationals crown. He had also won the season opener in 1975 in Super Stock.

Dave Settles had fallen short of victory in Pomona in Top Fuel in 1975 but went the distance two years later in Pro Comp with his injected nitro dragster.

1978

BROWN WINS FIRST ON SECOND WEEKEND

It took two wet weekends and a couple of days to complete the 18th annual Winternationals, but when the sun finally shone again on Pomona, it revealed a pair of familiar Winternationals winners in Don Prudhomme and Bob Glidden and a first-time Top Fuel champ in Kelly Brown.

After the first weekend was lost to rain, only one round of racing was completed the second Sunday before rain forced action to Monday, when another round went in the books before the day was lost to more rain and a bizarre dusting of hail and snow. The race finally was completed Tuesday, and for the second time in four years, as in 1975, Winternationals wins proved a springboard to world championships for the event's three Pro champs.

Brown, who had collected runner-ups in Top Fuel, Funny Car, and Top Gas, scored his first Pro win by ending the Cinderella bid of Washington's Gordon Fabeck, who was making his debut in Dean Rowley's new entry. Brown, who would handily win the season championship in the Donovan-powered Jim Brissette/Mike Drake entry, qualified No. 2 and beat Jeb Allen, Shirley Muldowney, and Rick Ramsey en route to the final. Don Garlits set low e.t. at 5.77, and Richard Tharp posted top speed at 250.69 mph.

Prudhomme scored his fourth straight Winternationals Funny Car title and milestone 25th NHRA national event triumph without crew chief Bob Brandt, who was in the hospital for back surgery. Although he qualified just third with a 6.17 (at 240.67 mph, top speed of the meet), behind low e.t. driver Tripp Shumake (6.157) and former mentor Tommy Ivo (6.159), "the Snake" had the quickest run of every round of eliminations in beating veterans Ed McCulloch, Gene Snow, and Tom McEwen and capped the victory with a solo pass after Ivo's machine broke a rod on its pre-run dry-hop burnout in the final.

Glidden led a record-quick Pro Stock field (8.90 bump) with his Pinto at 8.59, then he quickened the pace to a new track record of 8.56 for low e.t. Glidden's final-round opponent was defending event champ Larry Lombardo in Bill Jenkins' Chevy Monza, whom Glidden defeated decisively, 8.67 to 8.78, for his 13th Pro Stock title. Warren Johnson set top speed at 158.45 mph.

Tom Ridings scored in Pro Comp against favored Billy Williams to lead the Sportsman winners, who also included first-time champs Jim Mederer (Modified), Ron Zoelle (Super Stock), and Jeff Powers (Stock), and Wayne Clapp, who collected his fifth win in Comp.

Due to persistent rain, the 1978 Winternationals took two weekends and a few days to complete. The event finally was completed Tuesday of the second week.

Kelly Brown, a five-time national event runner-up in three classes, scored his first win to kick off a season that would conclude with him as the Top Fuel world champion.

Tommy Ivo, Top Fuel runner-up at the 1964 Winternationals, waited 14 years to return to the final, this time in Funny Car, only to split the engine on his dry hop against Prudhomme.

(Above) Don Prudhomme remained unbeaten in Winternationals competition for the fourth straight year. His Army-sponsored Funny Cars won 16 straight rounds in Pomona from 1975 to 1978. (Left) Bob Glidden won the Winternationals Pro Stock title for the third time in four years, besting defending event champ Larry Lombardo in the final. Glidden won the Winternationals seven times.

NOICE, HOOVER, GLIDDEN SHINE DESPITE RAIN

Veteran Southern California Top Fuel racer Bob Noice celebrated his reunion with longtime partner Jim Brissette by winning just his second national event title, and Tom Hoover and Bob Glidden posted wins in Funny Car and Pro Stock to highlight the season opener.

Noice, Top Gas champ at the 1968 NHRA Finals in Tulsa, Okla., landed in the fourth spot during rain-shortened qualifying with a 5.96, the last of four qualifiers in the fives, joining Gary Beck, Shirley Muldowney, and Jeb Allen. Noice never ran quicker than 6.03 in eliminations, but he got past some of the most competitive drivers in the field, including Larry Dixon Sr., world champion Kelly Brown, and Muldowney, whom he beat on a holeshot in the semifinals, 6.03 to 6.02. In the final, Noice cruised to the title after Rob Bruins couldn't start his car (his crew discovered a stripped fuel line coupler). Bruins would win the 1979 Top Fuel championship without the benefit of a national event win.

Hoover, who would finish sixth in the tough Funny Car competition in 1979, began the year with a final-round victory over Raymond Beadle's Blue Max. Following preliminary round-wins against Tom McEwen, Billy Meyer, and Tripp Shumake, Hoover drove his Showtime Corvette to a 6.29 in the final after Beadle, who had qualified No. 1, smoked the tires as soon as he hit the throttle.

The Funny Car field featured many of the day's biggest stars, such as Don "the Snake" Prudhomme, Gordie Bonin, and Gary Burgin, but did not include Kenny Bernstein, Dale Pulde, or "Big Jim" Dunn, who each suffered a rare DNQ largely due to the rain-shortened qualifying.

In the midst of a winning streak that would lead to nine straight national event victories, Glidden debuted his tiny yet potent Plymouth Arrow with a convincing win. Qualifying a full five-hundredths ahead of second-place Lee Shepherd, Glidden was a full two-tenths better than each of his race-day opponents, Mark Yuill, Larry Lombardo, Don Nicholson, and Joe Satmary, who put up a valiant fight in the final with an 8.71 but was no match for Glidden, who set both ends of the track record with an 8.49, 150.75.

The Pro Comp title went to Joey Severance, who survived a pair of big wheelstands in eliminations before defeating Jimmy Scott's small-block Chevy-powered dragster in the final. Dennis Ferrara (Comp), Dick St. Peter (Modified), Allan Patterson (Super Stock), and Jim Waldo (Stock) also made appearances in the Pomona winner's circle.

Bob Noice, who won Top Gas at the 1968 NHRA Finals in Tulsa, Okla., scored his first Top Fuel win in longtime friend Jim Brissette's The Other Guys dragster.

(Left) Nitro racing veteran Tom Hoover also scored his second victory when he drove his Showtime Corvette past tire-smoking Raymond Beadle in the Funny Car final. (Below) Longtime Ford campaigner Bob Glidden dominated Pro Stock with his Plymouth Arrow, qualifying No. 1 and winning his fourth of seven Winternationals crowns.

Beadle kicked off what would be his first Funny Car world championship season by qualifying No. 1 and scoring the runner-up.

Pro Comp winner Joey Severance was spectacular in victory, riding out a pair of wheelstands en route to winning his second Wally.

1980

Shirley Muldowney began what would be her second championship season by defeating former mentor Connie Kalitta to win Top Fuel.

Local hero Dale Pulde scored his second win when he piloted his and Mike Hamby's War Eagle Challenger to the Funny Car crown.

Six years after winning the Winternationals in Modified, Lee Shepherd collected his first of two Pomona Pro Stock crowns when he singled in the final.

(Above) Kenny Bernstein's debut in Budweiser colors looked good until the Budweiser King Arrow clouted the guardrail hard in the semifinals against Pulde. (Right) Larry Tores won the Winternationals three times in his fine Sportsman career. Four years after his Super Stock win, Tores won in Comp; he would do so again in 1986.

MULDOWNEY TOPS KALITTA IN MEMORABLE FINAL

Shirley Muldowney fired the opening salvo in one of the greatest rivalries in NHRA history as she beat her former teammate and mentor, Connie Kalitta, in the Top Fuel final. Longtime Southern California favorite Dale Pulde claimed a popular win in Funny Car, and Lee Shepherd downed surprise low qualifier Kevin Rotty to win the Pro Stock title.

Muldowney, who would win the second of her three NHRA world championships at the end of the season, made four straight runs in the fives during eliminations, including a 5.94 in the final to stun Kalitta, who was appearing in his first Pomona final since 1967. Driving her familiar pink dragster, Muldowney also beat Mark Oswald, Dave Uyehara, and John Kimble.

Pulde, who with Mike Hamby formed one of the most competitive teams of the 1980s, emerged from a tightly packed Funny Car field to claim the season-opening victory in his War Eagle entry, which had recently been re-bodied from a Trans Am to a Challenger. After knocking off Jim Dunn and Hank Johnson, Pulde was involved in a scary semifinal race against Kenny Bernstein, who hit the guardrail with his Budweiser Arrow. Pulde avoided contact with Bernstein and maintained his steady pace in the final with a 6.25 to stop Ron Colson, who, much like Bernstein, got out of shape. Colson, in Roland Leong's King's Hawaiian Bread Dodge, avoided contact but was disqualified after he crossed the centerline.

In the early stages of a brief but spectacular Pro Stock career that would include 26 wins and three world championships, former Modified ace Shepherd won for the second time in Pro Stock as he wheeled the venerable Reher-Morrison-Shepherd Camaro to a coasting win on a single run after Rotty, who had qualified No. 1 and set a new speed record at 160.71 mph, broke the rear suspension in his semifinal win against Frank Iaconio. Shepherd, the third-quickest qualifier with an 8.51, scored his biggest win of the day in the semi's when he topped Bob Glidden's Arrow, 8.61 to a slowing 8.95. Rotty had earlier benefited from a bit of good fortune as Bill "Grumpy" Jenkins and Iaconio both fouled against him.

The Pro Comp final pitted Brian Raymer's supercharged dragster against the Dark Horse Mustang Funny Car of Chicago's Fred Hagen. Raymer won with a 6.67 after Hagen smoked the tires. Other winners were Larry Tores (Comp), Jim Stevens (Modified), Don Brown (Super Stock), Jeff Powers (Stock), and Bob Tietz (Super Gas).

MEYER SURVIVES TEXAS CHAINSAW MASSACRE

Beginning a season that would culminate in a world championship, Jeb Allen won the Top Fuel title, and Billy Meyer and Bob Glidden claimed wins in Funny Car and Pro Stock, respectively, during the 1981 edition of the Winternationals.

The Funny Car final ended with Meyer taking a 6.52 to 6.66 win against fellow Texan Raymond Beadle, but it was a minor miracle that either made it to the starting line. After his semifinal victory against still-winless John Force, Meyer's Hawaiian Tropic Citation was in pieces as his crew hastily replaced a broken engine. However, the Meyer camp was relatively calm compared to

Beadle's pit area, where the crew and every available helper were busy grafting a new roof onto the body of the Blue Max Omni. The roof was graciously donated by Kenny Bernstein, who allowed the Blue Max team to virtually destroy his spare Budweiser King Arrow body. For Meyer, the win was just his second against Beadle in eight meetings.

Allen, who was just 17 when he burst on the scene with a semifinal finish at the 1971 World Finals in Ontario, Calif., was a polished pro by the time he defeated Marvin Graham in this final, 5.92 to 6.01. Allen, the No. 4 qualifier, posted runs in the 5.8s and was rarely challenged in eliminations; the

only opponent even close was Dave Settles, who was still nearly a tenth behind with a 5.94.

Glidden whipped the rest of the Pro Stock field with a string of low-8.3 clockings from his small-block Ford-powered Fairmont. He qualified No. 1 with a five-hundredths cushion on the rest of the field, which included national event winners Frank Iaconio, Lee Shepherd, Pat Musi, "Dyno Don" Nicholson, Ray Allen, and Butch Leal.

Glidden didn't let up on race day with 8.4s that none of his opponents could match. Paired with Musi's Camaro in the final, Glidden won easily, 8.38 to 8.52. The win was Glidden's fifth at the traditional

season opener, and he would claim two more Winter-nationals victories during his Hall of Fame career.

Jerry Darien, who with partner Ken Meadows has helped launch the careers of many promising young nitro racers, including Brandon Bernstein and Ashley Force Hood, claimed the Top Alcohol Dragster win against Brian Raymer, and Brad Anderson scored in Top Alcohol Funny Car by defeating Chuck Beal. Other winners were future Pro Stock crew chief Gary Pearman (Comp), Mike Edwards (Modified), Val Hedworth (Super Stock), Bill Bushmaker (Stock), and Scott Kendig (Super Gas).

(Above) Billy Meyer defeated fellow Texan and perennial nemesis Raymond Beadle to win in Funny Car and claim his fourth of 12 national event wins. (Below left) Jeb Allen kicked off what would be his most successful season by winning the Winternationals Top Fuel title, which served as a springboard to his only world championship.

It took an unprecedented roof transplant for Beadle to make the final; he had damaged the body of his Blue Max flopper in the semi's.

Bob Glidden won Pro Stock at the Winternationals for the fifth time, scoring from the No. 1 spot with his Ford Fairmont.

Jerry Darien, who has helped launch the careers of many of today's stars, scored in Top Alcohol Dragster for his only national event win; he was the event runner-up in 1976.

1982

Popular New Jersey pro Frank Iaconio won the first NHRA event for 500-inch Pro Stock cars and left Pomona with a 7.822 national elapsed time record.

Lee Shepherd recorded the first official seven-second Pro Stock run in NHRA competition. Besides Iaconio, Bob Glidden and Rickie Smith were also in the sevens at the event.

Dick LaHaie won the first of his two Winternationals Top Fuel titles after Shirley Muldowney broke in the final. LaHaie also won the Pomona opener in 1988.

Frank Hawley began his march toward back-to-back Funny Car world championships when he qualified No.1 and reached the semifinals in the famed Chi-Town Hustler.

NHRA founder Wally Parks, left, congratulated Al Segrini following his Funny Car victory. Segrini drove his Super Brut Dodge to a title-round win against Raymond Beadle.

MOUNTAIN-MOTOR PRO STOCKERS MAKE DEBUT

Dick LaHaie and Al Segrini scored popular wins in Top Fuel and Funny Car, respectively, but the highlight of the event was undoubtedly the adoption of 500-cubic-inch engines as the standard in Pro Stock.

Two pair into Thursday's first qualifying session, Lee Shepherd posted the first seven-second elapsed time with a 7.86 in the Reher-Morrison-Shepherd Camaro, and by the end of the event, three more drivers — Frank Iaconio, Bob Glidden, and mountain-motor veteran Rickie Smith — had joined him. Every driver in the field qualified with an e.t. quicker than the existing national record of 8.23 by Glidden, but none was quicker than Iaconio, who registered a historic victory when he defeated Shepherd in the final round, 7.83 to 8.02. Iaconio also left Pomona with the new elapsed time record, a 7.822 that he posted in the opening round.

Compared to the record-setting Pro Stock show, the Top Fuel final was rather anticlimactic. Shirley Muldowney lost fire on the burnout, allowing LaHaie to take a 6.11 single for the championship. Muldowney had run a string of 5.7s and was considered the favorite with a tenth advantage against LaHaie, who had qualified 14th and never ran better than 5.88 in eliminations. Despite the loss, Muldowney quickly recovered and finished the season by winning her

third Top Fuel world championship. Next to LaHaie's victory, the biggest story in Top Fuel was the performance of Australian Jim Read, who claimed the top spot with a 5.69 behind the wheel of R.J. Trotter's entry.

Segrini, who won three of his five titles in Pomona, grabbed his first with a 6.26 to 6.32 win against Raymond Beadle's Blue Max in the Funny Car final round. The eighth-quickest qualifier, Segrini drove his show-quality Super Brut Dodge to wins against Tom Ridings, Gary Burgin, and surprise semifinalist Doc Halladay. Beadle, the reigning Funny Car world champ, was one of three qualifiers in the five-second zone and reached the final round following a great 5.97 to 5.96 holeshot win against Frank Hawley in the famed Chi-Town Hustler. Hawley and tuner Austin Coil were not originally going to attend many NHRA events, but they changed their minds following their Pomona performance, which included a 5.86 for the top spot in qualifying. Shedding their reputation as match racers, Hawley and the Chi-Town team won back-to-back world championships in 1982 and 1983.

In the dragster versus Funny Car showdown that decided the overall Pro Comp title, Bill Barney drove his Broker dragster to a final-round win against Chuck Beal. Other champions were Bill Maropulos (Comp), Greg Smith (Super Stock), Jim Meyer (Stock), and Gary Cooke (Super Gas).

A WEEK LATE BUT STILL GREAT

It took an extra week to finish due to rainy weather that completely washed out half of qualifying and final eliminations, but the 23rd edition of the Winternationals came to a thrilling conclusion with popular Pro wins by Shirley Muldowney, Frank Hawley, and Frank Iaconio.

Muldowney, with her pink Top Fuel dragster carrying a big No. 1 on the rear wing, began her third title defense with a final-round victory against Jody Smart. Muldowney admittedly struggled during the event's first weekend but regrouped to qualify third, though she and everyone else were well off the pace set by Gary Beck, whose 5.52 was a full quarter-second quicker than No. 2 qualifier Smart's run. Beck reached the semifinals but shook the tires, allowing Muldowney to enter the final as the favorite with a 5.68. Smart, who had defeated Frank Bradley, Gene Snow, and Jerry Ruth, put up a good fight but smoked the tires and slowed to a 5.92.

After shocking the sport by earning the Funny Car world championship the previous season with their admittedly underfunded team, Hawley and the famed Chi-Town Hustler crew returned to Pomona and again proved their ability to defy the odds. Due to the challenging and ever-changing weather and track conditions, very few Funny Cars were in the five-second zone, but the Austin Coil-tuned Dodge was one of them, qualifying No. 2 with a 5.97 and

recording three straight 5.93 runs during eliminations against Don Prudhomme, Tom McEwen, and final-round opponent Tom Anderson. Anderson, driving Jim Wemett's Mercury, had the quickest car in qualifying with a 5.88 but slowed to a 6.02 in the title round.

For the 63 events that separated the 1979 Mile-High NHRA Nationals in Denver from the 1985 NHRA Southern Nationals in Atlanta, only four drivers — Bob Glidden, Lee Shepherd, Iaconio, and Warren Johnson — won in Pro Stock, so few should have been surprised to see Iaconio defeat Glidden in the Pomona final. The top two qualifiers with runs of 7.82 and 7.83, respectively, neither driver had much difficulty reaching the title round, although Glidden did get a reprieve when Shepherd fouled away a 7.85 in round two. After running as quick as a 7.79 on race day, Iaconio brushed aside Glidden's Ford, 7.81 to 7.99.

Al DaPozzo and Darrell Gwynn, two East Coast Top Alcohol Dragster racers who made the trip to Pomona, reached the final, where DaPozzo's Evil Spirit entry prevailed. Low qualifier Chuck Beal ran the table in Top Alcohol Funny Car, stopping Ed Grekul in the final, and Coleman Roddy (Comp), Ron Filkins (Super Stock), Bob Lambeck (Stock), and Ted Seipel (Super Gas) also collected wins.

After breaking in the final a year earlier, Shirley Muldowney returned to drive her Pioneer dragster to the Top Fuel title against Jody Smart.

Returning to Pomona as the reigning Funny Car world champ, Frank Hawley thrilled the fans with a trademark Chi-Town Hustler half-track burnout.

Frank Iaconio scored the first of two Winternationals Pro Stock titles when he beat Bob Glidden in the final. Iaconio also made the quickest run of the event, 7.80.

Future crew chief Tom Anderson qualified in the top spot in Funny Car with a 5.88 and wheeled Jim Wemett's Mercury-bodied entry to a runner-up finish.

Gary Beck's 5.52 run in Top Fuel qualifying was more than two-tenths of a second quicker than that of the next-quickest qualifier, Smart.

ORMSBY WINS FIRST; GARLITS RETURNS

Gary Ormsby, whose résumé would eventually include a world title, claimed his first Top Fuel win, and Al Segrini and Lee Shepherd also triumphed at the 24th opener, an event that, like many before it, played out before a packed house.

Ormsby's weekend began on a scary note when his car lost the rear wing at the end of a 5.73 run, but he stopped the car without incident. Ormsby and Joe Amato put on a great show in the final as they crossed the finish line just inches apart; the popular Northern California car dealer claimed a narrow win, 5.66 to 5.67. The Top Fuel finalists were nearly upstaged by "Big Daddy" Don Garlits, who returned to NHRA competition after a lengthy absence. Staging one of his many miraculous comebacks, Garlits upended low qualifier Gary Beck in round one, then downed longtime rival Shirley Muldowney before the clock struck midnight against Amato in the semi's. The appearance proved to be a sign of things to come as Garlits made another return several months later in Indy and won, helping to revitalize the Top Fuel class.

Segrini exploded a supercharger in a big ball of fire in the Funny Car final but was comfortably ahead of Tim Grose's Spirit Firebird. Driving his Super Brut Pontiac, Segrini, who would return a year later to defend his title, caught a break in the semifinals when he won a tire-smoking pedalfest against John Force. Kenny Bernstein was the early performance leader with a 5.83 but lost to Force in the opening round. Segrini's fireball was spectacular, but not nearly as frightening as the explosion and accident that sidelined popular Southern California driver Mert Littlefield in qualifying. Littlefield made contact with the guardrail, rupturing the fuel tank in his Littlefield & Bays Dodge Omni. The explosion ripped the body off the car, but Littlefield stopped it and climbed out, uninjured.

Shepherd took his first step toward the 1984 Pro Stock world championship when he beat Frank Iaconio in the final. Using consistent 7.7 runs to get past Roy Hill and Don Coonce, Shepherd drove the Reher-Morrison-Shepherd Camaro to a semifinal win against Bob Glidden, who fouled, then defeated Iaconio in the final, 7.71 to 7.76. Pro Stock fans had plenty to cheer for as class veterans "Dyno Don" Nicholson and Ken Dondero, both of whom were making their first starts in a 500-inch Pro Stock car, qualified for Sunday's eliminations.

Bruce McDowell and Hank Johnson headlined the list of Sportsman champions with respective wins in Top Alcohol Dragster and Top Alcohol Funny Car, and reigning champ Coleman Roddy (Comp), Dave Meredith (Super Stock), Vic Hobbs (Stock), and Alan Fillebrown (Super Gas) also visited the winner's circle.

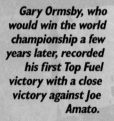

Gary Ormsby, who would win the world championship a few years later, recorded his first Top Fuel victory with a close victory against Joe Amato.

An engine explosion sent Mert Littlefield on a wild ride during Funny Car qualifying, but the popular Southern Californian was not injured.

In front of a packed house, Al Segrini downed Tim Grose to win his second Pomona Funny Car title in three years.

The latest round of the classic and often-repeated Lee Shepherd versus Frank Iaconio Pro Stock final went to Shepherd, far lane, 7.71 to 7.76.

Off the NHRA tour for the better part of two seasons, "Big Daddy" Don Garlits made one of his many successful comebacks, posting a strong semifinal finish.

SEGRINI LIGHTS UP THE SKY ONCE AGAIN

Trailing a shower of sparks behind Joe Pisano's JP-1 Dodge when his clutch let go in the lights, Al Segrini captured his second consecutive Winternationals Funny Car title with a thrilling final-round win against Dale Pulde. World champions Joe Amato and Bob Glidden also captured victories, in Top Fuel and Pro Stock, respectively, at a chilly Pomona event that was highlighted by record-setting performances.

In a scene eerily reminiscent of his win a year earlier, Segrini lit up the night sky as he cruised to a 5.78 victory against Pulde, who smoked the tires. Pulde, who would return to win the event in 1988, turned in a solid effort that included wins against Billy Meyer, John Force, and Ed "the Ace" McCulloch. Although he didn't score the victory, Rick Johnson shared some of the spotlight after driving Roland Leong's Hawaiian Punch Dodge to a 5.588, the first 5.5-second Funny Car run.

The racing in Top Fuel was no less exciting as Amato and "Big Daddy" Don Garlits, who would eventually combine for eight world titles, staged one of the best races of the year in the semifinals. At the start, Amato's dragster launched into a big wheelstand, but he never lifted. At the finish, Amato lifted the supercharger in a big ball of fire but crossed the finish line first as Garlits, who was leading at half-track, pitched a blower belt and slowed.

His Tim Richards-led crew working quickly to replace the damaged engine, Amato returned to post a 5.55 to 5.64 win against Gary Ormsby in the final. Amato had qualified with a 5.48 but was well off the pace set by Larry Minor, who had recorded a sizzling 5.43, then one of the quickest runs in the class.

With 7.6-second passes still a rarity in Pro Stock, Glidden continued to decimate the competition with performances that put him in a class by himself. He ran off a string of seven 7.5s, including a best of 7.53 in the opening round; his next-closest competitor, Lee Shepherd, could run no quicker than 7.60. Predictably, Glidden had little trouble beating Warren Johnson in the final, 7.58 to 7.77, and went on to win four more events during the season and the world championship.

The big performance numbers of 1985 weren't limited to the Pro classes: "Bad Brad" Anderson became the first Top Alcohol Funny Car driver to top 225 mph with a 6.32, 225.11 in qualifying and won the event.

Other champions included Dave Hage (Top Alcohol Dragster), Larry Kopp (Comp), Kip Martin (Super Stock), Bob Elliott (Stock), and Tom Turner (Super Gas).

Driving for legendary car owner Joe Pisano, right, Al Segrini captured his third Pomona Funny Car title in the last four seasons.

Switching from his EXP to a longer and more stable Thunderbird, Bob Glidden dominated the Pro Stock field with a string of 7.5-second runs.

Even a tire-smoking wheelstand wasn't enough to prevent Joe Amato from taking a semifinal Top Fuel victory against "Big Daddy" Don Garlits, who broke at half-track.

"Bad Brad" Anderson became the first Top Alcohol Funny Car racer to top 225 mph en route to his final-round win against Steve McGee.

Rick Johnson guided Roland Leong's Hawaiian Punch Dodge to a 5.58 in the quarterfinals to become the first Funny Car driver to run in the 5.5s.

1986

Other than Bob Glidden, the only Pro Stock driver to win in a Ford under the 500-inch rules is Frank Iaconio, who drove his Thunderbird to a win against Warren Johnson.

(Left) A young Darrell Gwynn, right, celebrated his Top Fuel victory with his father, Jerry, left, and NHRA founder Wally Parks. (Below) Tim Grose emerged as a leading contender in Funny Car after putting his Skoal Bandit Trans Am in the winner's circle by defeating John Force.

Future Top Fuel and Funny Car world champion Gary Scelzi collected his first victory when he beat Rick Santos in the Top Alcohol Dragster final.

The debut of Gary Ormsby's Top Fuel streamliner did not go as planned. He exploded a supercharger as soon as he hit the throttle in the burnout box.

IACONIO SCORES RARE FORD PRO STOCK WIN

With the notable exception of Bob Glidden, who spent much of his Hall of Fame career behind the wheel of a Ford Pro Stock car, no one else had much success with the blue-oval brand since NHRA switched to the 500-inch format in 1982. One driver who bucked the trend was Frank Iaconio, who gave up a promising career with a GM entry to join the Budweiser Superteam and was rewarded for two years of hard work when he put his Thunderbird into the winner's circle at the 1986 Winternationals. Darrell Gwynn also kicked off the season with a victory, in Top Fuel, and Tim Grose found the winner's circle in Funny Car.

After missing the field a year earlier, Iaconio qualified solidly with a fifth-best 7.58, just a few hundredths behind low qualifier Joe Lepone. On race day, Iaconio caught a break in the semifinals when Butch Leal fouled, then finished the job in the final round with a 7.56 after Warren Johnson got loose in his Olds and slowed from his earlier 7.5-second pace to a 7.77.

Top Fuel qualifying began with a bang; literally, as Gary Ormsby's revolutionary streamliner exploded a supercharger in the burnout box the first time he stepped on the throttle. Ormsby, who would be the 1990 NHRA Top Fuel world champ, failed to qualify the radical new entry. While Ormsby sat out Sunday's eliminations, Gwynn, in his second season of Top Fuel competition, won his first nitro title when he stopped Connie Kalitta in the final with a strong 5.46. The No. 4 qualifier behind Dick Lahaie, Shirley Muldowney, and Joe Amato, Gwynn did not have an easy draw as he was forced to beat Frank Bradley and his nemesis, "Big Daddy" Don Garlits, to reach the final.

With the backing of Skoal, Grose entered the 1986 season as a major player in the Funny Car class, and he wasted no time proving that as he cruised to his second victory. After topping low qualifier Kenny Bernstein in the semifinals, Grose lined up against John Force in the final, and although his vision was compromised by a fogged pair of goggles, Grose won by a 5.69 to 5.75 count. Force, who woudn't post his long-awaited first win for a year and a half, was relegated to runner-up for the sixth time despite a solid performance that included wins against Mike Dunn and Dale Pulde.

Sportsman winners were future Top Fuel and Funny Car star Gary Scelzi (Top Alcohol Dragster), Lou Gasparrelli (Top Alcohol Funny Car), Larry Tores (Comp), Smylie Little (Super Stock), Bill Bushmaker (Stock), and Scott Kendig (Super Gas).

'BIG DADDY' POSTS FINAL TOP FUEL WIN

They obviously had no way of knowing it, but the thousands of fans who streamed through the gates for the final day of the 1987 Winternationals will forever be able to say that they had the thrill of watching "Big Daddy" Don Garlits win what would be the 35th and final Top Fuel title of his illustrious driving career. Kenny Bernstein also turned in a dominating performance in Funny Car, and Warren Johnson reached the Pro Stock final round for the third straight year and scored his first Pomona victory.

Pushing his dragster only as hard as he needed to, Garlits never ran quicker than a 5.36 until the title round, where he turned up the heat and set the track record with a 5.29 to drive away from Joe Amato, who was several car lengths back despite a competitive 5.41 effort. Garlits, who hadn't won in Pomona since 1975, later proclaimed the victory a "modern-day miracle" as even he didn't expect to run within three-hundredths of the national record in the final.

Bernstein, who was racing his controversial "batmobile" Buick, so named for its gaudy aerodynamic enhancements and its sparse resemblance to its street-going counterpart, was in a class by himself in Funny Car. Qualifying four-hundredths ahead of the field with a track record 5.48, Bernstein unloaded a 5.49 in the title round on Aussie Graeme Cowin, who smoked the tires. Cowin, who had long ago proved that he was on par with the best drivers and tuners in the States, was trying to become the first non-North American to win an NHRA Pro title, and he nearly did it with upset wins against Raymond Beadle, Tim Grose, and John Martin. With each passing round, Cowin gained more fan support, drawing a loud ovation each time his crew sped down the return road proudly displaying the Australian flag from the roof of its push truck.

Well on his way to becoming a dominant force in Pro Stock, Johnson opened the season with a convincing victory. After qualifying second behind Bob Glidden, W.J. posted a string of 7.4-second runs in his Firenza to reach the final, where he downed Butch Leal, 7.43 to 7.52. Universally acknowledged as the master of the starting line, Leal won the first two rounds against Reid Whisnant and Glidden on holeshots and also left on Johnson in the final.

The other champions at the event were Denny Lucas (Top Alcohol Dragster), Chuck Phelps (Top Alcohol Funny Car), Todd Patterson (Comp), Val Hedworth (Super Stock), Harry Axemaker (Stock), and Ed Sellnow (Super Gas).

"Big Daddy" Don Garlits claimed the 35th and final Top Fuel title of his illustrious career with a dominating 5.29 to 5.41 win against Joe Amato.

(Above) Graeme Cowin and his Australian team made a lot of new fans in the States when they advanced to the Funny Car final with the Aussie Raider.

Warren Johnson won his only Pro Stock title of 1987 by driving his Olds Firenza to a final-round win against Butch Leal.

(Above) Cowin's bid to become the first non-North American to win an NHRA Pro title ended in the final round against Kenny Bernstein, far lane. (Left) Tim Morgan had a few tense moments in qualifying when he rolled his Top Fueler, but he did not suffer any major injuries.

(Above) In his first race as the reigning Top Fuel world champion, Dick LaHaie, far lane, posted a final-round victory against Joe Amato, who smoked the tires. (Right) Teamed with car owner and crew chief Bill Schultz, Southern California native Dale Pulde and the In-N-Out team scored an upset win in Funny Car.

(Above) After qualifying eighth, "the California Flash," Butch Leal, drove past several quicker opponents to pick up the Pro Stock title in his Rod Shop Pontiac. (Below) Beginning one of the most dominant years of his career, Pat Austin recorded the first of eight national event wins in his Castrol GTX Top Alcohol Funny Car.

Tripp Shumake heated up Funny Car qualifying when he suffered a fire in Billy Meyer's Chief Auto Parts entry.

LAHAIE BEGINS TITLE DEFENSE WITH WIN

Helping to dispel the myth of the "championship hangover" that has been known to stall many a title defense, 1987 Top Fuel world champ Dick LaHaie began the 1988 season with a convincing victory. LaHaie, long hailed as one of drag racing's working-class heroes and equal parts tuner and driver, wheeled his dragster to a final-round victory against Joe Amato in front of a packed house.

LaHaie's victory was popular, but fans also reveled in the Funny Car and Pro Stock wins by two native Californians, Dale Pulde and the original "California Flash," Butch Leal.

With Top Fuel cars beginning to frequent the 5.0-second zone, anticipation ran high for the sport's first four-second pass, but the bright sunshine and warm temperatures simply wouldn't allow it. Whatever was lacking in performance was more than made up for in quality as the stacked field also included former and future world champions Shirley Muldowney, Gary Ormsby, and Eddie Hill as well as Larry Minor, Gene Snow, and Darrell Gwynn.

LaHaie was never anything other than one of the favorites as he used a consistent string of 5.2-second runs to reach the final, where he set low elapsed time in the fading light with a 5.13 while Amato's dragster went up in smoke.

Off the tour for a couple of seasons, Pulde was driving a cement truck when he got a call from Funny Car owner and tuner Bill Schultz to drive his entry. Seizing the opportunity, Pulde made a string of consistent runs while each of his opponents, including Mike Dunn and John Force, smoked the tires. In the thrilling final with Jim Head, both entries were smoking the tires heavily by midtrack; Pulde recovered to gather his fourth title. Six hours after clutching the Wally, he was back behind the wheel of his cement truck.

All three Pro classes featured an unusually large number of upsets, especially in Pro Stock, where low qualifier Bob Glidden was ousted in round one by upstart Morris Johnson Jr. and Warren Johnson fouled against Tony Christian. Leal and Mark Pawuk qualified eighth and 11th, respectively, but made their way to the final, where Leal, long known for his quick left foot, grabbed a lead at the start and never looked back with a 7.45 while Pawuk, who had defeated Larry Morgan and Darrell Alderman, broke a rocker arm and shut off.

The roster of Sportsman winners included Mike Troxel and Pat Austin, who would go on to win national championships in Top Alcohol Dragster and Top Alcohol Funny Car, respectively, as well as Steve Taylor (Comp), Duane Jacobsen (Super Stock), reigning national champ Jim Waldo (Stock), and Dick Whitman (Super Gas).

1989

HILL, KALITTA ARE BIG STORIES AT RAIN-DELAYED EVENT

A pair of spectacular occurrences snared headlines at the 1989 season opener in Pomona, and they had little to do with who was celebrating in the winner's circle at the conclusion of the two-week rain-deferred event.

Gary Ormsby won Top Fuel, Bruce Larson scored in Funny Car, and Bob Glidden kicked off the season with a Pro Stock win, but the victories were somewhat overshadowed by Top Fuel racer Eddie Hill's stunning top-end somersault crash Friday and Connie Kalitta's 291.54-mph blast Saturday morning that christened him the first racer to break the 290-mph barrier.

During Friday qualifying, the front wings on Hill's dragster slipped into an upright position as he approached the finish line, lifting the front end. As air got under the nose, lifting it even higher, the rear wing tripped the clocks at 5.210, 236.15, then the dragster did a back somersault, rolled right-side up, and struck nose first, deploying the parachutes and slowing as it tumbled down the track. Remarkably, Hill suffered only bruised knees and returned to action in a car borrowed from Darrell Gwynn to qualify for the event and make an amazing comeback.

Ormsby didn't have the quickest or fastest car in Pomona, nor the most spectacular, but consistency won the Big Go West. Ormsby and his Lee Beard-tuned rail turned in a collection of the most consistent Top Fuel runs to that point in history and

won the race spectacularly with eight bracket-like 5.0 passes and a final-round defeat of Frank Bradley.

Funny Car winner Larson set low e.t. of the meet with a then-career-best 5.32 and expired three engines on his way to claiming his second career win, utilizing the career-best run to defeat first-round opponent and the category's then-winningest driver of all time, Don Prudhomme. In round two, Larson disposed of local racer John Martin, then got a free pass when Jim White was a no-show in the semi's. Kenny Bernstein smoked the tires in the final, and Larson sailed to victory.

Glidden emerged from Pro Stock qualifying in a shaky position, earning a start from the No. 5 position despite engine issues and changing "everything on that car but the driver," said Glidden. The change worked to his advantage, and he stopped Mark Pawuk in a close first-round race, put away Don Beverley in round two, and defeated nemesis Warren Johnson in the semi's. In the final, Glidden clicked off a track record 7.29 to defeat Frank Iaconio for his 68th victory.

Other event winners were Cruz Pedregon (Top Alcohol Dragster), Pat Austin (Top Alcohol Funny Car), Steve Taylor (Comp), Abe Loewen (Super Stock), Al Corda (Stock), and Dave Meziere (Super Gas).

Gary Ormsby, near lane, had the most consistent Top Fuel car at the 1989 event. He ran a 5.07 to end Shirley Muldowney's day in round one and followed with winning 5.07, 5.05, and 5.06 shots.

Eddie Hill's mind-boggling, heart-stopping top-end blowover in Friday's Top Fuel qualifying was a crash many veterans described as the most spectacular in the 29-year history of the event.

After crossing the finish line at 275 mph without parachutes in the first round, John Force sped through the shutdown area and flipped his Funny Car onto its roof in the sand trap.

Bob Glidden, near lane, beat Frank Iaconio in the Pro Stock final with a track record 7.29.

On Saturday morning of week two of the rain-delayed event, Connie Kalitta fired a shot heard 'round the drag racing world when he became the first racer to break the 290-mph barrier with a 291.54 blast.

UPSETS ABOUND AT FIRST EVENT OF THE DECADE

After windstorms and rainstorms led to a one-week delay, a new decade of NHRA Drag Racing opened with a trio of upsets at the 1990 event: Second-year driver Lori Johns ousted Dick LaHaie to become the third woman to win an NHRA Top Fuel title, Funny Car rookie K.C. Spurlock scored over a tire-smoking Ed McCulloch, and perennial Pro Stock middle runner Jerry Eckman put away Bruce Allen in one of the closest finals in history.

Johns drove her Jolly Rancher Candies dragster past Eddie Hill, Don Prudhomme, and Kenny Bernstein before facing LaHaie in her first final. After near-identical reaction times, .082 (Johns)

and .083, Johns ran a 5.031 to defeat LaHaie's 5.035 by just .005-second.

"We crossed a big hurdle," said Johns. "Last year, we were so much in awe of where we were and what we were doing. We were happy just to qualify and make it to the second round, but over the winter, we decided we needed to move on. We couldn't be in awe of Dick LaHaie and Kenny Bernstein forever. We had to tell ourselves we could beat them."

Former alcohol racer Spurlock, who switched to Funny Car after just one year in the alcohol flopper ranks, had completed licensing only nine days before the event and pulled off a huge stunner by putting away No. 1 qualifier

John Force, veteran R.C. Sherman, and defending series champion Bruce Larson en route to the final, where he stopped McCulloch.

"I never dreamed something like this would happen to me," said Spurlock. "We had some serious clutch problems last week, and we weren't even close to getting into the program until the last qualifying session. Then it rained, and we had another week to work on the clutch. We were out at the track every day by 9 o'clock, and we stayed until sundown. If we'd had to run the first round last week, the best we could have run was a high 5.4."

Eckman, who failed to qualify at nine races the season prior, qualified No. 1 and had

low e.t. in three of four rounds of Pro Stock eliminations. He got the best of 10-time national event titlist Allen in the final with a .002-second-quicker reaction and a 7.339 to 7.339 to win by just three-thousandths.

"I told myself, 'If I make the final, I ain't losing,' " said Eckman. "I thought he was in the car with me; it was that close. I was trying to size up our bodies to see who was ahead, and there was no doubt I had won, no doubt."

Other event winners were Blaine Johnson (Top Alcohol Dragster), Cruz Pedregon (Top Alcohol Funny Car), David Nickens (Comp), Ron Zoelle (Super Stock), Rob Robinson (Stock), and Ted Kellner (Super Gas).

(Above) Jerry Eckman led Pro Stock by qualifying No. 1 and dominating with his Pennzoil Pontiac Trans Am, which ran the quickest e.t. of every round except the second, where it shook in 1st gear. (Below) Johns' only gift during eliminations was a triple-zero red-light by Kenny Bernstein, who launched into a big wheelstand.

(Above) Lori Johns earned the distinction of becoming just the third female driver to win a Top Fuel title at the 1990 event. (Above right) In his first race behind the wheel of a nitro Funny Car, just nine days after completing his license, K.C. Spurlock pulled off a stunning upset and claimed his first Wally. (Right) Eckman, Johns, and Spurlock made up a trio of upset winners at the wild season opener.

BRADLEY, PRUDHOMME BACK ON TOP

Winning the 1976 Winternationals was the perfect launch to incredible seasons for nitro kings Frank Bradley (Top Fuel) and Don Prudhomme (Funny Car). Prudhomme went on to win seven of eight races that year, and Bradley's victory prompted him to become a full-time racer. When the two met in the Top Fuel final at the 1991 season opener, it seemed like a promising omen for both, no matter the outcome.

Bradley earned a start from the No. 11 spot, and low qualifier Prudhomme blazed his way into the Cragar Four-Second Club with a 4.98 best.

Race day was plagued with traction troubles beneath the hot sun, and the Top Fuel final was no exception. Bradley's car tried to spin the tires, forcing him to backpedal, while Prudhomme's mount lost a fuel line and hosed down the tires. Bradley recovered and roared to his second Winternationals title and fourth win of his career.

"This is my favorite track," said Bradley. "I got my start here, and it looked like I was going to get my finish here, too. If we didn't do well, I think we probably would have called it quits after Phoenix."

Defending Funny Car champion John Force held off Glenn Mikres and the Joe Pisano Olds in the final to win his 12th Wally. The hot and sticky surface made getting down the track quite a feat, but Force took the points lead after pedaling through tire shake against Art Hendey and Chuck

Etchells in their respective first and second-round matches, driving past Ed McCulloch in a superb semifinal duel, and taking the edge off the starting line and charging to victory after Mikres broke a fuel-pump shaft and the blower made a fiery exit.

"After so many losses, you get it right," said Force. "It's like when you first start going out on dates: After you blow it six or seven times, you start to get it right. That's where we're at right now."

Darrell Alderman got a hall pass to the top end when Warren Johnson's car broke behind the starting line in the Pro Stock final.

"I could feel the car lay down halfway through the burnout," said Johnson, then a 21-time winner. "I knew something was wrong."

Alderman inched toward the staging beams and zeroed in on the Tree.

"You get yourself mentally prepared in the second right before you race, and you don't notice what's going on around you," said Alderman. "When Buster [Couch, starter] comes into view holding up one finger [indicating a solo run], it's a weird feeling. I won't lie; it was a relief."

Other event winners were Rick Santos (Top Alcohol Dragster), Bob Newberry (Top Alcohol Funny Car), Rick Kelly (Comp), Ron Filkins (Super Stock), Bill Bushmaker (Stock), and Doug Bracey (Super Gas).

(Left) Frank Bradley had all but given up on racing due to sponsorship woes, but with encouragement and assistance from his racing friends, he brought out his rail for one last hurrah — and won. (Below) Don Prudhomme's 4.96 in testing was ruled not valid for membership in the Cragar Four-Second Club, but he locked up the second-to-last spot with a 4.98 in qualifying.

(Above) Darrell Alderman singled to the Pro Stock title after Warren Johnson had engine problems behind the starting line.

(Above) No. 3 qualifier John Force claimed his 12th victory, which kicked off his second straight championship season. (Left) After licensing in a Top Fuel dragster a week prior, Cruz Pedregon made his nitro debut at the event.

1992

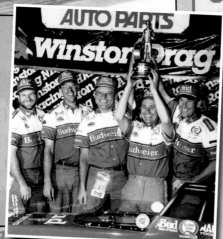

(Above) Jim Epler's Mike Kloeber-tuned Daytona, near lane, shocked the Funny Car troops with an upset victory over reigning world champion John Force in the final. (Right) After a rough Top Fuel qualifying outing bookended by a fireballing first pass and a blower-exploding last shot, Kenny Bernstein laid a big holeshot on opponent Jim Head en route to victory.

(Above) Jerry Eckman, far lane, who a round earlier had set the Pro Stock national record with a 7.17 blast, defeated Jim Yates with a 7.19 in the final.

The Top Fuel national record was reset by second-year driver Doug Herbert, who put a 4.88 on the scoreboards in the first round of eliminations.

A RECORD-SETTING START

Great weather and new concrete launchpads set the stage for a record-setting season opener in 1992: The Top Fuel e.t. national record was reset twice, Top Fuel and Funny Car boasted record fields, Top Fuel had a record nine four-second qualifiers and 25 four-second passes, and the Pro Stock e.t. national record was broken.

All classes put on extraordinary displays for the swelling crowds, but Top Fuel was the show of shows. Kenny Bernstein beat Jim Head in the final for his seventh title in a digger in the previous 19 starts and the 37th victory of his career, but he did so coming from the 11th qualifying position. The star on race day was second-year Top Fuel driver Doug Herbert, who recorded the quickest pass in history in the first round, a 4.880, breaking the 4.893 national record set in qualifying by Pat Austin.

"After we ran 4.97 [Saturday] night, I knew there was some left in the car, but I was looking more for a 4.95," said Herbert. "I knew the car was on a good run because it was smooth from start to finish. I just didn't know it was that good."

Former Top Alcohol Funny Car racer Jim Epler began his nitro Funny Car career at the Winternationals the year prior but lost in the first round and ran his car three more times that season without a round-win, so sweeping the 1992 opener was a bit of a surprise. Under the tune of Mike Kloeber, former crew chief for Don Prudhomme, Epler collected the upset win over world champion John Force in the final after putting away Richard Hartman, Al Hofmann, and Dale Pulde.

"The goal here was to get our team together, get them used to working with one another, and coordinate their efforts," said Epler. "We hoped to get in some good numbers and maybe get a semifinal finish. This is a real good class, and I think that at this race, you might've seen some of its future stars."

After rolling over former national event winners Kenny Delco and Bruce Allen with two of the better runs ever (7.21 and 7.20), Jerry Eckman, then Pro Stock's 10th-winningest driver, mopped the floor with the category's all-time king, Bob Glidden, in the semifinals with a record 7.17. Eckman pulled away from Jim Yates in the final to win by a car length.

"I guess this is about as good as it gets," said Eckman, the 1990 Winternationals titlist. "The only way this could have been better is if we had qualified No. 1, too."

Other event winners were Bernie Plourd (Top Alcohol Dragster), Bob Newberry (Top Alcohol Funny Car), Jeff Gillette (Comp), Ron Zoelle (Super Stock), Gary Sutton (Stock), Scotty Richardson (Super Comp), and Don Cumby (Super Gas).

BERNSTEIN WRECKS BIG; FORMER CHAMPS WIN

The winning 4.91 that defending Top Fuel world champion Joe Amato put on the scoreboard in the final at the 1993 opener was overshadowed by what was happening in the other lane: Kenny Bernstein was but a passenger in his Budweiser King rail as the engine blew in a violent ball of fire and smoke, and the resulting shrapnel appeared to shred the left rear tire and reduce the dragster to a pile of mangled metal.

Amato raced to the uncontested win while Bernstein fought for control of his flaming dragster as it shot across both lanes, steamed through the speed traps at 221 mph, and slammed into the right wall behind Amato and exploded on impact. Bernstein was dazed but

climbed from the wreckage of his own accord.

Two former world champions, Funny Car winner John Force and Pro Stock victor Warren Johnson, saw the spectacular display firsthand from the top end, where they were celebrating their event titles; Force had just won his second Winternationals title in three consecutive efforts, and Johnson earned his 35th victory with low e.t. of every round of qualifying and eliminations.

For Force, it was his first victory since Dallas the year before, and the win was particularly rewarding after a series of fires, crashes, and rollovers thwarted his campaign for the championship the previous season. Force made a day of beating opponents off the

starting line and came away victorious in the semi's on a holeshot over Dale Pulde in what was then the quickest side-by-side race in class history, 5.15 to 5.13. In the final, another holeshot secured the win in a close match with Del Worsham.

"It makes me feel good to win on driving ability," said Force. "The major deal was our car was consistent; it ran good numbers. What was here that we haven't had since Dallas was luck. Luck is the name of the game."

Reigning Pro Stock world champion Johnson picked up his fifth victory in six events by scoring a somewhat-predictable final-round triumph over nine-time runner-up Scott Geoffrion, who had chased his mentor in the points the bulk of the season

prior and ultimately finished second. A problem with the line-loc butchered Geoffrion's reaction, and Johnson got the nod despite inadvertently skipping 3rd gear and killing engine rpm.

In Sportsman action, Super Comp's Rod Hartzell claimed his first victory with the aid of a pair of perfect reactions and a .019 average launch throughout eliminations, and Top Alcohol Funny Car racer Lou Gasparrelli earned a long-time-coming second victory at the event where he earned his first seven years prior.

Other event winners were Brooks Brown (Top Alcohol Dragster), Ed Schuck Jr. (Comp), Rick Houser (Super Stock), Kenny Moore (Stock), and Paul Alabab (Super Gas).

Kenny Bernstein was leading Joe Amato and appeared to be on his way to a second consecutive Winternationals Top Fuel title before internal engine problems set off a chain of events that resulted in a spectacular crash.

For the third year in a row, John Force made his way to the Funny Car final round at the season opener. Force won in 1991 and was runner-up in 1992.

The Top Fuel title was awarded to Bernstein's opponent, Amato, who said, "I would rather he had won if it meant him not crashing. It takes the shine off the cake."

(Above) Popular local racer Lou Gasparrelli scored the second title of his Top Alcohol Funny Car career at the same event where he had notched his first seven years earlier. (Left) Pro Stock veteran Warren Johnson celebrated his 35th career victory at the event, and his son, Kurt, made his driving debut in the class.

1994

(Right) Then 28-year-old Shelly Anderson expertly rode out a punctured tire that sent her skidding across the finish line in a flurry of sparks to claim her second Top Fuel victory. (Below) Darrell Alderman, far lane, and Warren Johnson squared off in a highly anticipated Pro Stock final. Johnson was second off the line but won with the only 7.0 of the day.

(Right) Four years after kicking off his rookie Funny Car season with a win in Pomona, K.C. Spurlock returned after a three-year break to score at the opener again. (Below) Cruz Pedregon threw a scare into most of the Funny Car racers Thursday when he logged a track record and third-quickest e.t. of 5.01 and returned Saturday to crank out a 5.02.

Reigning Top Fuel champ Eddie Hill struggled at the season opener for the second year in a row, qualifying in the top half but smoking the tires in the first round.

ANDERSON, SPURLOCK WIN SECOND, W.J. 44TH

New talent and big sponsorships reinflated the Pro classes during the off-season and heightened expectations for one of the best years in the sport, and the 1994 opener didn't disappoint. Despite rain that hampered the first two days and threatened the last two, crowds converged on the Pomona facility in throngs and were rewarded with thrilling wins by Top Fuel driver Shelly Anderson, Funny Car racer K.C. Spurlock, and Pro Stock warrior Warren Johnson.

In Top Fuel, then five-time world champion Joe Amato ran the sport's quickest e.t., 4.751, in the first round but lost in the semi's, and the final pitted two drivers looking for a second win: Anderson and Rance McDaniel. Anderson qualified No. 3 with a 4.78, becoming the eighth driver to run in the 4.7s, and McDaniel, who collected his first Wally at the NHRA Finals three months prior, qualified fifth. In the wild final, McDaniel lost traction and almost crashed while chasing down Anderson, who appeared home free but lost the input shaft on her dragster just past half-track, which triggered a chain reaction of broken parts that shredded the right rear tire. She crossed the finish line the winner thanks to a superlative driving job combined with the tire-smoking trouble of her opponent.

Spurlock, the surprise 1990 Winternationals winner in his Pro debut, took a few years off from drag racing and returned in 1994 to duplicate his effort with a stunning final-round holeshot victory over Al Hofmann, 5.128 to 5.123. Though Spurlock was a sizable underdog heading into the event, he qualified third and easily made his way past a broken Gary Densham before beating Mark Oswald, 5.20 to 5.23. When semifinal opponent Kenji Okazaki was a no-show, Spurlock received a free pass to the third final of his Funny Car career.

Darrell Alderman issued a reminder of his potential for domination when he returned to Pro Stock racing after two years; the 1990 and 1991 world champion qualified second to former rival Johnson's No. 1 and eased his way through eliminations to their final-round meeting. The general consensus in the Pro Stock pits was that Alderman would leave first and Johnson would run quicker, thus pinning the outcome on the time it would take the latter to let out the clutch. As predicted, Alderman had .008-second on his opponent off the starting line, and Johnson lit up the scoreboard with the only 7.0 during eliminations to win by a narrow margin, 7.09 to 7.12.

Sportsman winners were John Shoemaker (Top Alcohol Dragster), John Weaver (Top Alcohol Funny Car), John Geyer (Comp), Art Peterson (Super Stock), Jim Waldo (Stock), Scotty Richardson (Super Comp), and Bob Button (Super Gas).

1995

HILL MAKES COMEBACK AT SUN-BAKED EVENT

Unseasonably low humidity and record-breaking heat didn't stand in the way of 1993 Top Fuel world champion Eddie Hill breaking a nearly 18-month win drought. Not only was it Hill's first victory since the 1993 Brainerd event, but it also was one of his most impressive triumphs to that point. Entering the event having made only two 300-mph runs, Hill defied the unusual conditions and exceeded the 300-mph barrier three times with a best of 304.05 and captured top qualifying honors with a 4.80.

After his winless year the season prior, Hill clicked off four consistently impressive times during eliminations, including a 4.85 conquest of then-reigning champion Scott Kalitta in the final round. Crew chief Fuzzy Carter changed nearly everything but the driver during the off-season and hunkered down to scrutinize data produced during the unlucky season. That was evidenced in every round Sunday and culminated in the final when Kalitta smoked the tires and Hill sailed to the long-awaited victory.

No. 2 Funny Car qualifier Cruz Pedregon was making his first start for the new McDonald's multi-car team of former NFL Washington Redskins coach Joe Gibbs and landed in his sixth consecutive final after getting past Gordie Bonin and Gary Clapshaw before edging Al Hofmann's identical 5.14 e.t. with a small holeshot in the semi's. In the final round, Pedregon took an easy — and lucky — win when Chuck Etchells stripped a clutch just off the starting line; Pedregon posted a non-stellar 5.30 at 278 mph for the victory.

Pro Stock teammates Darrell Alderman and Scott Geoffrion picked up where they left off in 1994: in the final, where Alderman again drove away from his Dodge teammate to score his 24th title. Qualifying certainly didn't indicate that it would be another Dodge Boys weekend; Warren Johnson was the class of the field, opening the season with a 7.13 that covered the field by three-hundredths and following with a track record 7.03 for a start from the No. 1 position. Alderman was two-hundredths behind Johnson going into race day, but the eventual winner had a car that favored a slight drop in temperature, and he outshone his opponents one by one to claim victory.

Top Alcohol Funny Car racer Randy Anderson's 1995 season began the same way 1994 ended, with a dominating Pomona victory and points lead. Other Sportsman winners were Bobby Taylor (Top Alcohol Dragster), Buddy Nickens (Comp), John Calvert (Super Stock), Chuck Rayburn (Stock), Les Figueroa (Super Comp), and Sheldon Gecker (Super Gas).

(Left) Eddie Hill ended a long drought when he defeated then-reigning Top Fuel world champ Scott Kalitta. (Below) Wally Parks, center, joined Funny Car winner Cruz Pedregon, second from right, tuner Bob Brandt, far left, and team owner Joe Gibbs, second from left, in celebrating Pedregon's victory in a third category.

In their second straight all-Mopar Dodge Wayne County final, Darrell Alderman, near lane, edged Scott Geoffrion, 7.05 to 7.10, for the Pro Stock title.

Defending Funny Car world champion John Force qualified in the top spot and unexpectedly fell in the second round.

(Left) Larry Dixon reached the semifinals of Top Fuel in his Pro debut 30 years after team owner Don Prudhomme won his first NHRA title at the same race.

1996

JOHNSON, HOFMANN, YATES NET WILD WINS

Seldom has a season begun with so much drama in the Professional finals alone as in 1996. Whether you wanted pyrotechnics, a full-fledged rivalry, or conspiracy theories, each Professional class had something in store.

Personal drama ensued in Funny Car when John Force and Al Hofmann, who respectively finished No. 1 and 2 in the championship standings in 1995, engaged in a heated final-round battle. Hofmann was able to drive his patched-up entry past his opponents after a first-round race against Mark Sievers, during which Sievers caught on fire and was unable to avoid Hofmann's car at the turnoff area. Beaten and bruised, Hofmann's team advanced to the final to face the juggernaut Force, who had

upset top-performing Cruz Pedregon in the semifinals. Pedregon had made the quickest and fastest runs in Funny Car history with a 4.934 at 307.06 mph during qualifying. Force was a thousandth off of a perfect light in the final round, but it didn't matter when he had to pedal while Hofmann cruised to victory. The dramatics from the racetrack spilled into the pressroom when a remark by Hofmann got under Force's skin and the two traded barbs.

Blaine Johnson began the 1996 Top Fuel season as he had ended the 1995 season — with a win. Johnson equaled the quickest run in class history with a 4.665 to take the No. 1 qualifying position. Johnson, the hottest young driver in the

class, met seasoned veteran Connie Kalitta in the final round. It was Kalitta's first final-round appearance since his historic U.S. Nationals win in 1994. Johnson won by posting low e.t. of eliminations with a 4.73 while all eyes were on Kalitta's lane. At the end of a worthy 4.82 at 297 mph, Kalitta's dragster erupted into a huge fireball, but he pulled his rail safely to a stop.

Jim Yates, the 1995 Pro Stock championship runner-up, was the main client of engine builder Richard Maskin, who had a number of cars in the field. Yates steamrolled past three Pro Stock greats in eliminations by defeating Bob Glidden, Kurt Johnson, and Warren Johnson. When Yates

put the finishing touches on W.J., 7.06 to 7.08, the other semifinal match was contested between Maskin customers Billy Huff and Chuck Harris, and Huff won on a Harris red-light. Yates ran a 7.04 in the final while Huff slowed considerably to a 7.14.

Rainy weather that had pushed final Pro eliminations to late Sunday also pushed the Sportsman finals to Monday for the first time since 1986. Eventual season titlists Bobby Taylor (Top Alcohol Dragster) and Tony Bartone (Top Alcohol Funny Car) emerged victorious. The other Sportsman winners were Dean Whittman (Comp), John Calvert (Super Stock), Eric Waldo (Stock), Marvin Rouse (Super Comp), and Mike Blodgett (Super Gas).

(Above left) Tony Bartone began a remarkable winning streak that led to a season title with a convincing Top Alcohol Funny Car win. (Above right) Jim Yates opened his first Pro Stock championship season with a win in his Pontiac. He defeated fellow Richard Maskin engine customer Billy Huff in the final.

Fresh off his long-awaited first Top Fuel win at the 1995 Finals, Blaine Johnson impressed by equaling the quickest e.t. in class history during qualifying and beating Connie Kalitta in the final.

Al Hofmann, near lane, beat rival John Force in the final despite a near-perfect .401 light (.400 Tree) by Force. The two traded barbs during Hofmann's post-race interview in the pressroom.

Hofmann, the 1995 Funny Car championship runner-up, began the year with a memorable win. His team had to make repairs on race day after first-round opponent Mark Sievers made contact with him at the top end while slowing from a fire.

SCELZI SCORES EMOTIONAL, HISTORIC WIN

A record weekend crowd witnessed a spectacular event in beautiful Southern California weather. All eyes were on a former alcohol racer Gary Scelzi, who was handpicked by Alan Johnson to take the controls of his Top Fuel dragster five months after Johnson's brother, Blaine, tragically lost his life in a crash during qualifying for the 1996 U.S. Nationals. The Top Fuel rookie did great with a 4.62 No. 1 qualifying effort, and his driving skills were put to the test on Sunday.

Scelzi saved a potential first-round loss by instinctively pedaling when the dragster lifted the front end too high. The second round was a performance-fest, in which all eight Top Fuelers ran 4.6 seconds or better. Shelly Anderson set the speed record at 316.90 mph in a losing effort, and Joe Amato looked to have the car to beat on Sunday with three straight 4.5-second passes, including a national record 4.56 that netted him a $35,000 bonus. Amato was poised to be the first driver to win running all 4.5-second elapsed times just one race after he became the first driver to do so with all 4.6s. But in the final, Scelzi beat Amato in a pedalfest. Amato lost a blower belt, and Scelzi scored an emotional win for the Johnson family with a 7.71 at 231 mph. Scelzi became the first driver since 1990 to win in his Pro debut.

John Force and unsponsored foe Al Hofmann

went at it again in a rematch of their 1996 final. Hofmann got his car back together after a nasty fire in the first session of qualifying on Thursday. After the first round, Force belted out three consecutive four-second passes. The final round was no contest when Hofmann's machine lost traction.

The Pro Stock final was a family affair. Warren Johnson and son Kurt raced each other in the money round for the first time since K.J.'s 1993 rookie season. W.J. set the national e.t. record at 6.927 seconds in the semi's, and Kurt took care of 1996 world champ Jim Yates with a holeshot win in the other semifinal round. Kurt was quicker on the Tree, but W.J. moved around him to win by .013-second, 6.96 to 7.00.

In Top Alcohol Funny Car, Frank Manzo scored the season-opening win in what would be his first of seven consecutive national championship years. Bobby Taylor defended his 1996 Top Alcohol Dragster Winternationals crown, and Bo Nickens (Comp), Gene Bichlmeier (Super Stock), Al Corda (Stock), Pat Mulligan (Super Comp), and Kevin McClelland (Super Gas) also took top honors.

Joe Amato and his Jimmy Prock-led Top Fuel team impressed by lowering the national e.t. record to 4.56 and posting a runner-up.

(Left) In an emotional day, the Johnson family returned to drag racing after the death of driver Blaine Johnson and won the event with Top Fuel rookie Gary Scelzi at the controls.

(Right) John Force avenged his 1996 loss to Al Hofmann by defeating him in the Funny Car final with his third straight four-second run. (Below) The father-son Pro Stock driving tandem of Warren and Kurt Johnson celebrated an exciting final in which W.J. held off the kid by .013-second.

A string of seven consecutive Top Alcohol Funny Car season titles for Frank Manzo began with a win for the New Jersey driver at this event.

1998

Reigning Pro Stock world champ Jim Yates netted his 18th victory in the third all-six-second field in class history.

Legendary driver Don "the Snake" Prudhomme celebrated his first double win as a team owner when Larry Dixon and Ron Capps took the respective Top Fuel and Funny Car titles.

(Right) The triumph of Dixon, second from left, and Prudhomme, second from right, was an immediate payoff for hiring legendary tuner Dale Armstrong, far right, and clutch wizard Bob Brooks, far left. (Below) Capps, near lane, used his pedaling expertise to halt a surging Tim Wilkerson in the Funny Car final.

(Right) Years after supporting the drag racing aspirations of son Shaun and daughter Tiffani, John Hyland joined them on the list of national event winners in his return to Top Alcohol Funny Car.

DIXON, CAPPS SCORE WINS FOR 'SNAKE'

Legendary drag racing figure Don "the Snake" Prudhomme had been, well, snakebitten in Pomona with no wins since his 1978 Winternationals triumph in Funny Car. His luck as a team owner didn't appear to be any better after his driving retirement at the end of the 1994 season until his pair of fuel drivers, Larry Dixon and Ron Capps, stepped up to win and earned their boss a pair of Wallys.

"I feel like Roger Penske," said an ecstatic Prudhomme.

It was a long road to get both Dixon and Capps to a level of competitiveness where a double-up win was a possibility. Neither driver had won a single round in the first three races of 1997, which was the first year of Prudhomme's Funny Car team. With Roland Leong having righted the ship on Capps' Funny Car and legendary tuner Dale Armstrong stepping in to guide Dixon's Top Fueler during the off-season, this team came into the season coiled and ready to strike.

Dixon scored his first four wins during his first 15 races in the 1995 season but had only scored one since and was hungry for more. Against Jim Head in the final, Dixon scored a holeshot victory, 4.75 to 4.73. Both drivers had trouble and didn't make it to the finish-line stripe under power.

Although Al Hofmann posted the quickest time in Funny Car history during qualifying at 4.862 seconds, performance didn't win this event in the late rounds. Awareness was key when Capps pedaled his tire-smoking entry past semifinal opponent Tony Pedregon and final-round nemesis Tim Wilkerson with respective elapsed times of 5.92 and 6.60.

Jim Yates took Pro Stock honors for the 18th time from the third all-six-second Pro Stock field in NHRA history. He beat youngster Jeg Coughlin in a great final round. Coughlin got off the line first but couldn't hold off Yates, who won by .002-second, 6.96 to 6.98. Coughlin, who beat Warren Johnson on a holeshot in the semifinals, netted a holeshot win in every race of his young Pro career.

Rick Santos, the 1997 Top Alcohol Dragster world champ, started the season with a win by beating Rick Henkelman's powerful A/Fueler. John Hyland made history in Top Alcohol Funny Car by joining son Shaun and daughter Tiffani on the list of NHRA national event winners. Future Funny Car driver Jack Beckman scored the first win of his career in the Super Comp ranks. Randy Jones (Comp), Mark Faul (Super Stock), Jim Meador (Stock), and Mike Ferderer (Super Gas) also scored victories.

DUNN, COUGHLIN STAR IN MONDAY FINISH

Rainy weather may have pushed eliminations beyond the weekend, but the cool temperatures that never exceeded 65 degrees set the stage for record-setting conditions in the Pro categories. The first fueler to run down the racetrack was that of Eddie Hill, who blistered the quarter-mile with a 4.53. That was only a sign of things to come.

Mike Dunn drove Darrell Gwynn's Ken Veney-tuned dragster to four consecutive 4.5-second runs on race day, including a national record 4.503 that netted him a $35,000 bonus. He earned the 17th win of his career by defeating defending event champ Larry

Dixon, who smoked the tires, in the final round, and he earned Gwynn his first victory since the 1996 Memphis event. Both of Dunn's Pomona wins occurred during the 1999 season.

Jeg Coughlin earned his sixth Pro Stock win in dramatic fashion. The young driver damaged the nose of his race car in the sand trap after winning in the first round, and chassis builder Don Ness worked hard to fix it between rounds. Coughlin advanced to the final by beating Rickie Smith and George Marnell on holeshots and posting a 6.91 against Kurt Johnson. In a team final, Coughlin met up with brother Troy, who had to abort his run and gave Jeg an

easy win with a 6.96.

The Funny Cars drew a great deal of attention with a field of drivers hoping to dethrone eight-time and defending world champ John Force and the arrival of dynamic personalities Jerry Toliver and Scotty Cannon, but the show was tough to predict; many heavy hitters exited early in eliminations.

Tony Pedregon may have notched one of his uglier wins when he slithered through the field amid a great deal of tire shake on each pass. His only representative run on race day was a 4.88 against Dean Skuza in the semifinals.

Winless final-round opponent Gary Densham got to the money round for the sixth

time with three six-second runs. Densham stepped up to a 5.04, but it wasn't enough as Pedregon drove around him with a 4.97.

Randy Daniels ran steady 7.6s to take the Pro Stock Truck crown and recorded a 7.65 to finish off Brad Jeter in the final. Larry Kopp qualified No. 1 and set the national e.t. record with a 7.58.

Rick Santos repeated as Winternationals champion in Top Alcohol Dragster. Bucky Austin (Top Alcohol Funny Car), Alan Freese (Comp), Jimmy DeFrank (Super Stock), Mark Faul (Stock), Jimmy Lewis (Super Comp), and Sheldon Gecker (Super Gas) took the remaining Sportsman honors.

Mike Dunn, right, and team owner Darrell Gwynn broke a three-year slump when they captured the Top Fuel title in impressive fashion.

(Left) Tony Pedregon, far lane, defeated a then-winless Gary Densham in the Funny Car trophy round. (Below) Jeg Coughlin, left, stopped his brother Troy in an all-family, all-Jegs Pro Stock final round.

Second-generation driver Randy Daniels joined his father, former Comp and Modified racer Garley Daniels, on the list of NHRA national event victors.

(Left) Winning in Pomona was a common theme during both of Jimmy DeFrank's Super Stock championship seasons. DeFrank won this event and the season title.

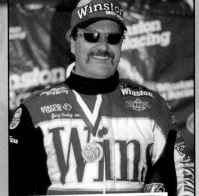

Gary Scelzi (right) made a winner's circle appearance at the Winternationals for the first time since his Top Fuel debut in 1997. (Below) Jerry Toliver won his second straight race when his Dale Armstrong-tuned Funny Car scored big in Pomona.

(Right) Jeg Coughlin looked like "Jeg the Unstoppable" when he opened the season with the Pro Stock victory for the second straight year and reached the final for the third straight. (Below) Ron Krisher walked away unharmed from a harrowing crash in the first round of Pro Stock in which Kurt Johnson's Chevy suffered damage when trying to avoid him.

Bob Panella Jr. nabbed the Wally in Pro Stock Truck with 7.5-second runs and a final-round triumph against Greg Stanfield.

NEW RULES A HIT AT SUCCESSFUL EVENT

NHRA Drag Racing changed forever at the turn of the millennium. Rules were put in place to limit the percentage of nitromethane in the tank to 90, establish penalties for oiling the racing surface, and allot 75 minutes between rounds. What resulted was a fast-paced event and consistent, side-by-side racing with few delays.

Coming off his first season as a Pro in which he didn't score the coveted season title, Gary Scelzi reached the Top Fuel final at this event for the first time since he won it in his rookie season. The two-time season titlist ran low e.t. of the meet with a 4.60 when defeating Larry Dixon in the semifinals. He had a shot to dismantle the efforts of Tony Schumacher at a repeat championship in the final round and did so by taking six-hundredths at the stripe in a 4.61 to 4.71 victory. It was the fourth Winternationals triumph for owner and crew chief Alan Johnson and the third for Scelzi.

Jerry Toliver's Funny Car got hot at the end of the 1999 season and continued with a second straight win. Legendary tuner Dale Armstrong made a shocking move back to the class after spending the entire 1990s wrenching on dragsters, and he propelled Toliver to four four-second runs in eliminations. Defending event winner Tony Pedregon had set a track record with a 4.83 in the semifinals, but Toliver compensated on the starting line in the final and scored a 4.97 to 4.92 holeshot victory.

Fresh off a five-win season that resulted in a championship runner-up, Jeg Coughlin advanced to the Pro Stock final for the third straight season. Coughlin made the quickest run of each eliminations round and handled the driver with the No. 1 on his window, Warren Johnson, with a 6.89 to "the Professor's" 6.95. The Pro Stock show provided a scare in the first round when Ron Krisher crashed his entry and Kurt Johnson grazed the wall trying to avoid him, but neither driver was harmed.

Bob Panella Jr. picked up the honors in Pro Stock Truck. He got the better of 1999 Auto Club NHRA Finals champ Greg Stanfield in the final, 7.54 to 7.58. Oddly, all four winners in the Professional categories did so from the No. 2 qualifying position.

Rick Santos continued his domination at this event in Top Alcohol Dragster with his third straight and fourth overall victory. Larry Miner took the Wally in Top Alcohol Funny Car by beating former Top Alcohol Dragster champ Jay Payne, and he was joined in the winner's circle by Bryan Morrison (Comp), Bill Bennett (Super Stock), Don Little (Stock), Kyle Seipel (Super Comp), and Bob Herr (Super Gas).

RUSSELL SHINES IN 50TH-SEASON KICKOFF

The celebration of the 50th season of NHRA Drag Racing began with a very special Winternationals. Reminders of NHRA's hot rod heritage were apparent throughout the event with nostalgic displays, such as a Cacklefest and a gathering of champions.

The NHRA Top Fuel Shootout had been postponed due to weather delays at the 2000 NHRA Finals and rescheduled for this event, adding excitement to an already exhilarating show. Former Top Alcohol Dragster racer Darrell Russell filled in for retired Top Fuel legend Joe Amato and performed remarkably in a runner-up finish to Gary Scelzi on Saturday. On race day, he did one better by winning the event. Not only was Russell a rookie but so was his crew chief, Jimmy Walsh, who had been a crewmember for Amato since 1985. Final-round opponent Mike Dunn had run three straight 4.63s in eliminations, but he went up in smoke in the final, and Russell ran a 4.66 for the win. Russell joined K.C. Spurlock (1990) and Scelzi (1997) on the list of drivers to win this event in their Pro debuts.

The Funny Car class was a battle, as evidenced by a record 5.013-second bump spot. Bruce Sarver, who was fresh off a runner-up finish at the NHRA Finals in Alan Johnson's Funny Car, made it to the final round from the No. 6 spot with a string of four-second runs. His combatant

was Tony Pedregon, who reached the Winternationals final for the third year in a row. Sarver got the best of him, 4.88 to 4.95, and picked up his second Wally.

Kurt Johnson, who won six of the last 12 Pro Stock races to close the 2000 season, ushered in the debut of the Chevy Cavalier in style. All eight of his runs were over 200 mph, including a class-best 202.18-mph blast. He made three 6.8-second runs in wins against Mark Osborne, Mike Edwards, and No. 1 qualifier Bruce Allen to meet Darrell Alderman in the final. Alderman had defeated Johnson's father, Warren, in the semifinals. K.J. nabbed the win with a 6.91 to Alderman's 6.93.

The 1999 Winternationals Pro Stock Truck champ, Randy Daniels, bounced back from a DNQ in 2000 to reach the winner's circle once again. He qualified No. 1 and set low e.t. with a 7.46. Daniels took care of Greg Stanfield in the final, 7.52 to 7.55.

Rick Santos won the Top Alcohol Dragster crown for the fourth consecutive season and fifth time in his career by beating Mark Hentges in the final round. 1999 winners Bucky Austin (Top Alcohol Funny Car) and Jimmy DeFrank (Super Stock) each won for the second time in three years. They were joined in the winner's circle by Jeff Lion (Comp), Australian transplant Bernie Cunningham (Stock), Larry Scarth (Super Comp), and Ed DeStaute (Super Gas).

(Left) Former Top Alcohol Dragster driver Darrell Russell won in his Top Fuel debut behind the wheel of Joe Amato's dragster, joining K.C. Spurlock and Gary Scelzi as the only other Pros to do so. (Below) The late Bruce Sarver kicked off the 50th season of NHRA Drag Racing with his second win with the Funny Car team owned by Alan Johnson.

Kurt Johnson, who won six of the last 12 Pro Stock races in 2000, kept his hot streak alive to win in the debut of the Chevy Cavalier.

(Above) Russell, far lane, nearly doubled up at his first event as a Pro. Before winning Sunday, he took Amato's place in the NHRA Top Fuel Shootout Saturday and made it to the final but lost to Scelzi. (Left) Five-time Lucas Oil champion Rick Santos won in Top Alcohol Dragster for his fourth straight and fifth overall Winternationals victory.

FANS EXPERIENCE SOME VERY REAL POWER

The first event of NHRA's POWERade era kicked off in grand style. Fans were treated to warm, sunny conditions and an onslaught of great racing.

The beer wars between respective Budweiser- and Miller-sponsored drivers Kenny Bernstein and Larry Dixon that took the spotlight during their 2001 championship battle waged further when the two met up again in the final round of the Winternationals.

There was no change in the pecking order as qualifying might have indicated; Andrew Cowin, who qualified No. 1 and set low e.t. with a 4.49, and Tony Schumacher, who set top speed with a booming 330-mph blast, both lost in the first round. In the first of many epic final-round encounters of the 2002 season, Dixon got off the starting line first and took a 4.53 to 4.61 victory.

John Force added anticipation to his quest for 100 wins by reaching No. 99 with his first Winternationals score since 1997. He set low e.t. with a 4.74 during qualifying, and teammate Gary Densham nabbed the national speed record at 326.87 mph. Force met a red-hot Del Worsham in the final round. Worsham, who won the 2001 NHRA Finals, bested his teammate, Johnny Gray, in the semifinals to meet Force. Both drivers lost traction in the final and engaged in a pedalfest that Force won, 6.26 to 6.64.

A wacky Pro Stock season that demonstrated parity at its finest began with a season-opening win by George Marnell, one of nine winners in the first nine races of the season. The Las Vegas construction mogul did an amazing job on the starting line, netting three of a possible four round-wins on holeshots. The door appeared open when 2001 season champ Warren Johnson lost in the second round and 2000 champ Jeg Coughlin failed to qualify. Marnell capped his fantastic day with a .417 light and a 6.88 elapsed time that held off Jim Yates' much-quicker 6.81.

Not unlike Marnell, Top Alcohol Dragster winner Steve Federlin got it done on the starting line. Federlin beat three of his four opponents, including runner-up Mark Hentges, on holeshots. The only eliminations round that Federlin didn't win on a holeshot was still decided on the starting line when Rick Santos red-lighted away a quicker e.t. in round two, ending his Winternationals winning streak at 17 rounds.

Pat Austin scored his 75th and, pending a comeback to the sport, final win of a storied racing career. Austin took the Top Alcohol Funny Car crown when his uncle Bucky Austin suffered a disintegrated clutch disc in the final. Mike DePalma (Comp), Dan Fletcher (Super Stock), Ken Passerby (Stock), Mike Ferderer (Super Comp), and David Coapstick (Super Gas) also took home wins.

Former Winternationals champ Mike Dunn helped welcome POWERade's series sponsorship with a thunderous burnout.

The beer wars were in full force when Larry Dixon, near lane, defeated Kenny Bernstein in the Top Fuel final.

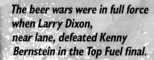

(Left) Pat Austin logged the 75th win of his illustrious career by defeating his uncle Bucky Austin in the Top Alcohol Funny Car final. (Above) George Marnell scored his biggest win when he used holeshots to beat three of his four opponents en route to a Pro Stock victory.

John Force ended his four-year absence from the Winternationals winner's circle by defeating Del Worsham in a pedalfest in the Funny Car final for career win No. 99.

DIXON DOUBLE HIGHLIGHTS RECORD WEEKEND

A weekend double that netted him $200,000 made Larry Dixon the star of a highlight-filled 43rd edition of the Winternationals, which also featured wins by Tony Pedregon and Warren Johnson and a pair of new national records.

Entering the 2003 season opener, no Top Fuel racer had ever won the Winternationals in consecutive years, but that changed when Dixon, the reigning world champion, obliterated the Top Fuel field.

Dixon began his dominant weekend with a $100,000 victory in Saturday's NHRA Top Fuel Shootout, which had been carried over from the 2002 season finale due to weather. It was Dixon's second straight win in the bonus event, making him just the third driver to go back to back.

He made more history Sunday when he wheeled his ride past Cory McClenathan to claim his historic repeat event win and the $50,000 double-up bonus.

Dixon, who won the final-round bout in a 4.54 to 4.59 decision, became only the second driver (with Joe Amato) to pull off the double and the first to earn the $50,000 NHRA bonus money.

Equally impressive were fellow winners Pedregon and Johnson, both of whom put on quite a show as they drove to respective wins in Funny Car and Pro Stock. Pedregon hammered the flopper contingent with 4.7-second run after 4.7-second run in eliminations, including a 4.739 in

round one that was the fourth-quickest pass ever recorded to that point. Pedregon was the only driver in the field to dip below the 4.80 mark Sunday and just the third in history to run all 4.7s on race day. In the final, Pedregon powered his John Force Racing Mustang to a 4.76 to handily defeat Johnny Gray, who was a distant second with a 4.91.

Johnson also lived in the .7s, the 6.7s, in eliminations as he picked up win No. 89, this one at the expense of Allen Johnson, whose 6.80 was no match for the .003-initiated 6.78 put on the boards by "the Professor" in the final. In addition to the Wally, Johnson left Pomona with a new national speed record after clocking a 204.91-mph run in the opening round.

The record-setting performances weren't restricted to the Professional classes. In Top Alcohol Dragster, Tony Bartone set a new national e.t. record at 5.22 seconds, and in the final, he defeated Morgan Lucas in the quickest side-by-side TAD race ever, 5.26 to 5.29. Other Sportsman winners were Doug Gordon (Top Alcohol Funny Car), Randy Jones (Comp), Jeff Lane (Super Stock), Mike Loge (Stock), Jack Beckman (Super Comp), and Brad Pierce (Super Gas).

After winning the NHRA Top Fuel Shootout bonus race, Larry Dixon went the distance in Top Fuel, becoming the second to pull off the double and the first to pocket the double-up bonus.

(Above) Tony Pedregon became just the third driver in history to run all 4.7s en route to victory in Funny Car, including a 4.739 that was the fourth-quickest run ever.

Warren Johnson's season got off to a good, fast start. "The Professor of Pro Stock" won the season opener and set a new national speed record of 204.91 mph.

(Above) Tony Bartone, near lane, became the ninth driver to win in both alcohol classes when he defeated Morgan Lucas, 5.26 to 5.29, in the quickest side-by-side TAD pairing in history. (Left) Future Top Fuel and Funny Car driver Jack Beckman notched his second national event win when he bested Geoff Hughes in the Super Comp final.

Greg Anderson (right) notched the first of 15 season wins with a dominating performance that included outpacing the Pro Stock field by three- to four-hundredths en route to victory. (Below) Jerry Toliver's return to Funny Car after a nearly two-year absence was a highly successful one, ending with his new team in the winner's circle.

(Right) After showing the way in Top Fuel performance the second half of 2003, Tony Schumacher picked up right where he left off at the 2004 opener, scoring win No. 12. (Below) Eric Medlen was impressive in his Funny Car debut. Tuned by father John, Medlen led qualifying until the final session, when boss John Force bumped him to second.

Perennial Stock contender Toby Lang was among the Sportsman winners. He defeated Bernie Cunningham to collect his ninth national event Wally.

ARMY TEAM, ANDERSON BEGIN DOMINATION

Tony Schumacher and Greg Anderson gave everyone a taste of what was to come the rest of the season when they grabbed respective wins in Top Fuel and Pro Stock during the rain-delayed 44th running of the Winternationals. Schumacher, Anderson, and Funny Car champ Jerry Toliver had to wait an extra week to claim their victories after rain soaked the area during the original event weekend, forcing a one-week pause.

Schumacher's and Anderson's victories at the opener were the start of record-setting seasons for each — a Top Fuel-record 10 wins for Schumacher and NHRA-record 15 wins for Anderson. Schumacher's domination actually had begun midway through 2003 when Alan Johnson signed on as his crew chief, and the dynamic duo carried its strong performance into the 2004 opener, where the U.S. Army team qualified No. 2 and rattled off three straight 4.4s to trailer Rhonda Hartman-Smith, David Baca, and Brandon Bernstein. The only round in which a 4.4 did not come up on Schumacher's scoreboard was the final, but that didn't matter because Doug Kalitta had engine problems on the starting line and couldn't make the run.

However, as impressive as the Schumacher win was, it paled in comparison to the show put on by Anderson. With the No. 1 emblazoned on his car after he secured his first world title the season before, Anderson completely demoralized the rest of the Pro Stock field with a performance that included grabbing the top qualifying spot, setting low e.t. and top speed of the meet, and consistently running four-hundredths or more ahead of the entire field as he dispatched Mike Corvo Jr., Mike Edwards, Larry Morgan, and Warren Johnson to score his 17th Wally.

Schumacher's and Anderson's wins could be classified as normal fare, but Toliver's triumph in Funny Car was far from it. After sitting on the sidelines for almost two years, Toliver stunned everyone when he claimed the title at his first event back. After having a tough go in qualifying and just making the show with a 15th-best 4.952, Toliver's new team came to life Sunday, running low e.t. (4.738) and top speed (328.22) on the way to victory. After defeating rookie Eric Medlen, Cory Lee, and Del Worsham, Toliver handily took care of Gary Densham in the final, 4.82 to 4.95.

The event's Sportsman titles went to Mitch Myers (Top Alcohol Dragster), Dennis Taylor (Top Alcohol Funny Car), Dean Carter (Comp), Abe Loewen (Super Stock), Toby Lang (Stock), and Bob Harris Jr. (Super Gas).

SURPRISES AND RECORD RUNS ABOUND

The 2005 season got off to an unexpected and quick start during a record-setting and surprising opener that featured victories by Scott Kalitta (Top Fuel), Tommy Johnson Jr. (Funny Car), and Dave Connolly (Pro Stock).

The tone for the much-buzzed-about affair was set early with quick qualifying sessions that resulted in a new national speed record in Top Fuel (Tony Schumacher, 334.65 mph), the quickest Top Fuel field ever with seven qualifiers in the 4.4s and a 4.59 bump, and the second-quickest Funny Car e.t. ever (Tony Pedregon, 4.681).

Though the pace slowed slightly on Sunday, the action was no less exciting as surprises were plentiful. After dominating the previous season, Schumacher was the favorite in Top Fuel, but an uncharacteristic driving error put him on the trailer in round two. In Funny Car, all three John Force Racing entries lost in the opening round, the first time in five seasons the team suffered that fate, and Don Schumacher Racing was shut out of the final for just the third time in 24 events. Pro Stock dominator Greg Anderson also struggled, qualifying seventh, his lowest start in two years, and losing in the second round.

The early exits by the favorites opened the door for some different faces to work their way to the final rounds, including Top Fuel finalists Kalitta and Doug Herbert.

Kalitta won the battle, capping an impressive day that included all 4.4-second runs, the first driver to run all 4.4s in eliminations, with a 4.48 to 5.37 win against Herbert.

In Funny Car, Johnson snapped a nearly four-year winless streak when he bested Phil Burkart Jr. in the final. After catching a lucky break in the opening round when opponent Frank Pedregon crossed the centerline on what likely would have been a winning run, Johnson ran three straight 4.7s, including a career-best 4.741 in the final against Burkart.

Connolly erased the memory of a miserable end to the 2004 season that included three straight early exits when he outlasted Warren Johnson, who also was coming off a tough close of the previous season with two nonqualifying efforts in the final six events. Connolly clearly had the car to beat on race day, running low e.t. or close to it in every round of competition when he worked his way past Jeg Coughlin, Allen Johnson, Ron Krisher, and Warren Johnson to land in the winner's circle.

The event's Sportsman titles went to Steve Federlin (Top Alcohol Dragster), Frank Manzo (Top Alcohol Funny Car), Michael Stone (Comp), Don Little (Super Stock), Mike Hiatt (Super Comp), and Steve Parsons (Super Gas).

Don "the Snake" Prudhomme's team gave him a fitting celebration for the 40th anniversary of his first NHRA national event win when Tommy Johnson Jr. scored in Funny Car.

Scott Kalitta, near lane, joined father Connie as a Winternats winner when he defeated Doug Herbert in Top Fuel. Kalitta was impressive en route to victory, running all 4.4s.

In a weekend of surprises, one of the biggest was Jim Yates, who took the Pro Stock pole after missing the field at half of the races the previous season.

(Above) Pro Stock newcomer Dave Connolly bested veteran Warren Johnson to pick up national event win No. 4 and take the points lead for the first time in his career. (Left) Tony Pedregon had an interesting Funny Car outing, making a trip to the sand after his pole-winning 4.681 Saturday. The team returned with a repaired car and went to round two.

Melanie Troxel, who previously won in Top Alcohol Dragster, became the eighth woman to win in a Pro class when she claimed the Top Fuel Wally over David Baca.

Robert Hight made a dramatic run to the Funny Car winner's circle, struggling to qualify, then catching on fire and burning up his Mustang body before claiming victory.

Greg Anderson put together another crushing performance in Pro Stock, qualifying No. 1, running low e.t. and top speed, and defeating Mike Edwards for top honors.

Hillary Will made her debut in Ken Black's Top Fuel dragster, and she made a strong first impression, qualifying fourth in the quick field. Fellow rookie J.R. Todd placed third.

Lou Ficco Jr. scored a wire-to-wire win in Comp, qualifying No. 1 with his B/AA Cavalier and defeating former national champ Dean Carter in the final.

TROXEL SCORES FIRST TOP FUEL VICTORY

Melanie Troxel added her name to the short list of women to win in NHRA's Professional classes when she defeated David Baca in the Top Fuel final to cap a weekend filled with many twists and turns and headlined by victories by Troxel, Robert Hight (Funny Car), and Greg Anderson (Pro Stock).

Though qualifying featured its share of exciting moments and big happenings — John Force posted the quickest Funny Car e.t. ever, 4.664, for example — the drama was at its peak on Sunday. In both fuel classes, none of the top-half qualifiers advanced past the second round, and the Top Fuel semifinals featured three drivers who had never won a national event. Also, three of the four Pro Stock semifinalists — Mike Edwards, Mark Pawuk, and Larry Morgan — didn't finish in the top 10 the season before.

Top Fuel was guaranteed a first-time winner when Troxel and Baca each advanced to the final round. Troxel won the battle with Baca, 4.58 to 8.67, to become the sixth woman to win in Top Fuel and the eighth in a Pro class.

Hight epitomized the dramatic nature of the event, going from struggling to qualify to winning the race. Though his Sunday went much smoother than the previous days, it wasn't without its excitement. As Hight crossed the finish line in the second round against Del Worsham, his engine let go, erupting in flames and destroying the body of the car. The body on the car for that run was actually the backup, so the team had to get a little creative to make repairs and return for the semi's. Hight's crew went to the show car in the Top Eliminator Club, removed the body, and took it back to the pits, where it was prepped to run on the car. The team got everything ready just in time for its semifinal match with Phil Burkart Jr. Hight won the pairing, then went on to defeat Ron Capps in the final.

In Pro Stock, the event went pretty much as expected: Anderson, who was coming off a third straight championship-winning season, swept the race. He qualified No. 1, ran low e.t. and top speed, and drove to victory on Sunday, defeating Bob Panella Jr., Rickie Smith, Morgan, and Edwards.

The Sportsman classes weren't free of surprises, the biggest of which came in the Top Alcohol Funny Car final when defending event champ Frank Manzo red-lighted to give the win to Jay Payne. Joining Payne in the Sportsman winner's circle were Duane Shields (Top Alcohol Dragster), Lou Ficco Jr. (Comp), Keith Lynch (Stock), Anthony Castillo (Super Comp), and Val Torres Jr. (Super Gas).

A STAR IS BORN DURING DRAMATIC OPENER

Though the wins by J.R. Todd (Top Fuel), Gary Scelzi (Funny Car), and Greg Anderson (Pro Stock) will forever be a major topic when discussing the 2007 opener, the event will also be remembered for the debut of the sport's next star, the return of a legend, and record performances.

Ashley Force Hood, daughter of 14-time world champ John Force, garnered most of the spotlight during the weekend when she made her first official runs as an NHRA Pro, and she certainly gave everyone something to buzz about. Force Hood qualified in dramatic fashion, entering the final session not in the Funny Car field and then bumping into it while moving her father out of the field in the process (he later bumped back in).

Also embroiled in the qualifying drama and crazy bumping was Kenny Bernstein, who made his return to the flopper class. His comeback didn't exactly go according to plan, though, as he failed to qualify.

Much of the drama associated with Funny Car can be attributed to incredible performances brought on by prime racing conditions. Robert Hight clocked the quickest time in history (4.646), Scelzi posted the third-fastest speed ever (333.49), and a 4.795 bump made the field the quickest in history. The Top Fuel field was also the quickest in history with a 4.575 bump, and in Pro Stock, Anderson

reset the track speed record at 209.04 mph.

Anderson's record was part of an absolutely perfect performance that resulted in a second straight Winternationals title. Anderson once again dominated the competition, qualifying No. 1, running low e.t. and top speed, and clocking the best time of every round as he dispatched Richie Stevens Jr., Mike Edwards, Dave Connolly, and Greg Stanfield.

Scelzi nearly matched Anderson's performance, qualifying No. 1, setting top speed, and winning the event. Scelzi faced Hight in the final round, and the race was a wild one. Hight left the starting line and crossed the finish line first for an apparent 4.72 to 4.71 holeshot win, but he was disqualified for crossing the centerline. That gave the win to Scelzi, who became the third driver to win the Winternationals in both nitro classes.

In Top Fuel, sophomore Todd used a string of 4.4s to claim his fourth victory. He defeated defending event champ Melanie Troxel, Doug Kalitta, and Dave Grubnic in the first three rounds, then powered to a 4.48 to best Brandon Bernstein in the final.

Winners in the Sportsman classes were Brandon Johnson (Top Alcohol Dragster), Jay Payne (Top Alcohol Funny Car), Jody Lang (Super Stock), Clark Holroyd (Stock), Tom Yancer (Super Comp), and Randy Fabbro (Super Gas).

(Left) Though she didn't win, Ashley Force Hood stole the headlines when she made her debut in Funny Car. The rookie qualified for the record field, placing 15th with a 4.790. (Below) Sophomore Top Fuel driver J.R. Todd notched his fourth win when he defeated Brandon Bernstein in the final. Todd ran three straight 4.4s en route to victory.

(Left) Gary Scelzi, near lane, won a wild Funny Car final over Robert Hight. Hight finished first in the match, but he crossed the centerline, disqualifying him.

As he had in previous years, Greg Anderson dominated Pro Stock, putting two 6.64s and two 6.65s on the boards on his way to the win.

Jay Payne was the final racer standing in Top Alcohol Funny Car for the second straight year, this time defeating Sean Bellemeur for top honors.

2008

JOHN FORCE AND TEAM STEAL THE SHOW

Tony Schumacher (Top Fuel), Robert Hight (Funny Car), and Greg Anderson (Pro Stock) won the season-opening event of 2008, but their victories were just a small part of the story-filled event in Pomona. John Force returned to action just months after suffering what could have been career-ending injuries in a crash in Dallas, Antron Brown made an impressive Top Fuel debut, Melanie Troxel had a strong showing in her first foray into the Funny Car class, and Tony Pedregon suffered an enormous engine explosion in the opening round that sent him on a wild and fiery ride, which made highlight reels on

newscasts across the country and landed the 2007 champ on NBC's *Today* show.

Hight's victory capped a great weekend for the John Force Racing team. Team owner Force made his return to the track and looked good doing it; his was one of three Force cars to make it to the semifinals, joining Hight and daughter Ashley Force Hood in the penultimate round. Though a win by Force would have been the ultimate storybook ending for the team, Hight's victory was also quite satisfying for the team because it came one year after Hight was on pace for a sure win but crossed the centerline and was disqualified. This event went much better for Hight; he defeated

Ron Capps, Gary Densham, Force, and Cruz Pedregon to claim the Wally.

It was business as usual in Top Fuel and Funny Car, in which regular winners Schumacher and Anderson made another visit to the winner's circle. Schumacher qualified third, then clocked low e.t. of each round to dispatch Doug Kalitta, Doug Herbert, Larry Dixon, and Cory McClenathan and claim his 42nd Wally, which put him second on the all-time wins list.

Anderson won his third straight Winternationals title and did so in the same fashion as the previous two, using utter domination to crush the field. He qualified No. 1 with a 6.62, 209.39-mph run that reset the track speed record, then clicked

off a series of passes between 6.61 and 6.64 to defeat Johnny Gray, Greg Stanfield, Allen Johnson, and rival Jeg Coughlin.

Though he did not win the race, Brown had a strong first go in Top Fuel, qualifying No. 1 and advancing to the second round. Troxel nearly joined Brown as a low qualifier, coming within a session of nabbing the top spot in her Funny Car debut. She held the No. 1 spot through three sessions before being bumped down to third.

Winners in the Sportsman classes were Duane Shields (Top Alcohol Dragster), Frank Manzo (Top Alcohol Funny Car), Jim Cowan (Comp), Dan Fletcher (Super Stock), Toby Lang (Stock), and Kyle Seipel (Super Comp).

(Above) Robert Hight celebrated in the winner's circle with team owner John Force, who was making his return to competition after he was injured in an accident late in 2007. (Right) After qualifying third, Tony Schumacher ran low e.t. of every round to place his U.S. Army-backed rail in the winner's circle for his 42nd victory.

(Above) Antron Brown made a seamless transition from Pro Stock Motorcycle to Top Fuel, qualifying No. 1 and winning the first round in his debut. (Left) Greg Anderson won his third straight and fourth overall Winternationals title, sweeping the event with a No. 1 start, low e.t. and top speed, and a final-round defeat of Jeg Coughlin.

After winning the final three national events of 2007, Dan Fletcher continued his winning ways when he claimed the Super Stock crown. Fletcher also advanced to the Comp final.

RAIN TURNS RACE INTO WEEKLONG AFFAIR

The 2009 Winternationals will long be remembered not for the tight racing and victories by Doug Kalitta (Top Fuel), Ron Capps (Funny Car), and Jason Line (Pro Stock) but instead for being one of the longer events contested in NHRA history after taking seven days to complete. Rain dogged the first five days, eliminating all but one of the Professional qualifying sessions and pushing eliminations from Sunday, when one round was completed, to Monday and then ultimately to Tuesday for the Pros and Wednesday for the Sportsman racers.

The wait was well worth it for Kalitta, who joined uncle Connie and cousin Scott as a Winternationals winner. The win was a much-needed pick-me-up for Kalitta, who had gone more than a year since his last trip to the winner's circle. Starting from the No. 11 spot, Kalitta defeated Urs Erbacher, Cory McClenathan, and Morgan Lucas in the opening stanzas. In the final, Kalitta won a tight battle with Antron Brown, 3.82 to 3.84, to earn career win No. 31.

Capps also erased a win drought of more than a year when he defeated Jim Head to claim the Funny Car title. Capps earned his Wally in strong fashion, powering to low e.t. in three of the four rounds, including a 4.054 that stood as the best time of eliminations. After defeating John Force, Bob Tasca III, and Robert Hight in the first three rounds, Capps got the nod in the title round when Head lost traction at the hit of the throttle.

Line scored the fifth win for his KB Racing team in six years when he bested Mike Edwards in the Pro Stock final, 6.56 to 6.57. Line, the No. 2 qualifier behind teammate Greg Anderson, earned his final-round date with Edwards when he trailered Rickie Jones, Johnny Gray, and Allen Johnson in the first three rounds.

Line's win capped an incredible day of performances that included new track records, numerous personal bests, a new national e.t. record (Anderson's 6.528), and a near miss on the speed record when Line posted the second-fastest time ever, 211.63, on a run where he botched a shift.

The Sportsman racers had to wait an extra day to wrap up competition, but there were story lines aplenty when the race concluded. Tony Bartone's return to Top Alcohol Funny Car ended in victory, Dan Fletcher followed up his 2008 Super Stock triumph with a Comp win, and John Calvert wheeled his new Cobra Jet Mustang to victory in Stock. Joining the trio in the Sportsman winner's circle were Jim Whiteley (Top Alcohol Dragster), Shane Studley (Super Stock), and Justin Lamb (Super Gas).

(Above) Connie Kalitta's 50th year in drag racing got off to a great start when nephew Doug scored in Top Fuel to claim his first Winternationals title. **(Left)** Ron Capps snapped a 41-race win drought, and he did so in fine fashion, running low e.t. in three of the four Funny Car rounds, including a weekend-best 4.054.

The Summit team's dominance at the Winternationals continued with another win and a new national record. Jason Line (above) added a fifth win in six years for the team when he bettered Mike Edwards in the final, and teammate Greg Anderson set the national e.t. record at 6.528 (right).

Forty years after a Cobra Jet Mustang won at the event in its debut, the feat was repeated when John Calvert drove his new 40th anniversary Cobra Jet to victory in Stock.

My Most Memorable WINTERNATIONALS

JIM DUNN

The Long Beach, Calif., native is a current Funny Car owner and crew chief, and he has competed at the Winternationals since its infancy. He reached the final round in Middle competition in 1963 and Top Fuel in 1966.

"[Co-owner Al] Yates and I were runner-up to [Mike] Snively in the Top Fuel final in 1966. Even though we didn't win, we put on the quickest side-by-side drag race in history at the time. It was a lot of fun back then because you did everything by yourself and could try anything you wanted. The staging lanes weren't organized then, so you'd see people lined up eight lines across all the way out the back and make one run all day. Some people would sneak to the front of the staging lanes by sleeping in their trailers and rolling their car out at 5 a.m. You'd see people do things like change oil while in line and get in fistfights with people who wouldn't move."

CONNIE KALITTA

The legendary driver has been in five Winternationals finals since 1963, and he scored his sole win in 1967. Late son Scott (2005) and nephew Doug (2009) are also Top Fuel champs at the event.

"Until I won Indy [in 1994], a few races stood out as the biggest races I've ever won, and that includes the '67 Winternationals. Prior to that, my biggest win was at the '64 Smokers meet in Bakersfield, which had a 32-car field in Top Fuel. I'd been going out west for races from Michigan since '59. Being on the road sure was a lot of fun back then. What stands out the most in my mind from that year was winning 'the triple crown' by winning the Winternationals in three different sanctioning bodies: NHRA, IHRA, and NASCAR."

DON GARLITS

"Big Daddy" Don Garlits brought Swamp Rat V to Pomona in 1963 to claim his first of 35 NHRA Top Fuel wins. The event was the first in several years at which nitromethane use was permitted.

"I went to Bruce Crower's shop as I always did when we came to that area, and he suggested that we build a wing over the engine to give the lightweight, 120-inch-wheelbase car some more traction. They didn't pass it through tech inspection the first time, so they sent me through the reject line, where they called [NHRA's] Jack Hart over, and he said, 'Garlits, this is the craziest thing I've ever seen, but it doesn't look like it's going to be dangerous. We'll just let you run it, and everyone can have a nice laugh.' The Pomona track was a little slick, and [Art] Malone and I started marching through the field. Malone is a little heavier, which helped with traction on the rear wheels. We were even at the eighth-mile, and the pressure from the wing started kicking in and helped me pull away. It was my biggest win at that time."

DON PRUDHOMME

"The Snake" won the Winternationals five times from 1965 to 1978 in three classes and has won five times as a team owner, including a double victory with drivers Larry Dixon and Ron Capps in 1998.

"I think the first one is always the best one, and my first one was in the Hawaiian car with Roland Leong and Keith Black. If you won the Winternationals or the U.S. Nationals in those days, it really put you on the map, and we won both of them. It was a huge deal for Roland and me because the notoriety from it was strong enough for us to book our car around the country in match races and allowed us to become professional racers. It was like being a prize fighter. Heck, in those days, Ford gave away a pickup truck with a camper at the U.S. Nationals, which was a big deal for us. We also got a Ford cammer engine [when we won the Winternationals]. We took the money offered instead of the engine, and to this day I wish I kept that engine."

SHIRLEY MULDOWNEY

GARY SCELZI

The three-time Top Fuel world champ and 2005 Funny Car world champ has won the Winternationals in three classes: Top Fuel (twice), Funny Car, and Top Alcohol Dragster. He posted his first Top Fuel win in his Professional debut in 1997.

The Winternationals has featured some of the great moments in the career of the legendary three-time Top Fuel world champion, including her wins in 1980 and 1983.

"I have quite a few memorable moments, but the first win with the Top Fuel team was obviously the biggest one ever. It was pretty incredible racing guys like Kenny Bernstein, Joe Amato, Connie Kalitta, and Cory Mac [McClenathan]. It was neat meeting them, but once I got in the car, I just tried to do everything right and not make Alan [Johnson, crew chief] mad. In the first round against Spike Gorr, the car went into a wheelstand, and I pedaled it to run a 4.80-something and win the round. I did the world's worst pedal job in the final and still managed to get the win. I told Alan that we won our first two races together, and I still didn't have any idea what was happening when I was driving. Obviously I did, but it took 50 runs before I was sure."

"It was great to blow [Connie] Kalitta off in the final when we won Pomona in '80. On top of that, we rolled a brand-new Attebury car out of the trailer. We really detailed the appearance of the car, and we scheduled it so tight that the paint was still wet. [Don] Garlits came over to the trailer and said, 'I've gotta take a look at this con-traption.' We had low e.t. with a 5.83 and went on to win the race. I remember our wins in '80 and '83 well and cherish them. I had the car to win it in '82 as well, but it stalled at the end of the burnout in the final because of the way the main fuel line was shaped, and I watched [Dick] LaHaie win with a miserable run that was a half-second slower than mine. I gave it to him."

TEN MEMORABLE DEBUTS

The axiom "technology marches on" is as true today as it was in 1961, when the Winternationals, by its very position on the annual schedule as the NHRA season kickoff, became the event where new technology often debuted. Though the event also is known for driver and sponsor unveilings, many memorable technological and new-car developments have been introduced at the event. Here are 10 of the more memorable.

1961: Nicholson's 409 Stocker

Legendary quarter-mile racer "Dyno Don" Nicholson had one of the first vaunted Chevrolet 409 engines beneath the hood of his '61 Chevy at the first Winternationals. Nicholson's victory, recounted on page 62, earned the 409 tremendous popularity among the drag racing faithful who hung on the results of every Stock race as do today's Top Fuel and Funny Car fans. The shock waves were felt all the way to Detroit and led Ford and Pontiac to counter with similar engines in 1962, the former with tri-power 406-motivated Galaxies and the latter with 421-powered Catalinas, though Nicholson again held sway with his oh-so-fine 409.

1963: Garlits' Swamp Rat V Top Fueler

Lacking the tires and clutch systems to harness the power of their nitro-fueled engines, the lightweight Top Fuelers typically made passes smoking the tires the entire quarter-mile. Don Garlits added a large airfoil to his 1,200-pound Swamp Rat V at the 1963 opener, hoping to gain much-needed downforce. Garlits said that NHRA Competition Director Jack Hart called the wing "the most obnoxious-looking thing I've ever seen," to which Garlits countered, "Jack, when the smoke clears, every dragster in competition everywhere will have a wing on it someday. Trust me." Garlits won the race to post his first of 35 NHRA titles, and though smoke-free runs were still a few years away and wings a few more, there's no arguing his foresight.

1968: Cobra Jet Super Stockers

In the late 1960s, NHRA Super Stock racing was virtually dominated by Chrysler Corp. and its mighty 426 Hemi engines. The Mopar contingent got a nasty surprise at the 1968 season opener when Ford Motor Company unveiled its Cobra Jet Mustangs. Ten cars, prepared especially for NHRA Super Stock racing by the Holman, Moody and Stroppe organization in Long Beach, Calif., entered the battle, and at the end of race day, Al Joniec, driving the Rice-Holman entry, had emerged victorious following a string of mid-12-second elapsed times.

1971: Garlits' Swamp Rat 15 Top Fueler

Though rear-engine Top Fuel dragsters had been tried, usually with less than successful results, it again took Don Garlits to get it right. During his rehabilitation from an early-1970 transmission explosion in his front-engine Swamp Rat 13 that severed half of his right foot, Garlits designed what would become the first successful rear-engine dragster. After off-season testing to work out handling problems, Garlits won the Winternationals and forever changed the face of Top Fuel.

1972: Jenkins' Grumpy's Toy IX Vega Pro Stocker

In its infancy, Pro Stock was a big-block affair, with 426 Hemis doing much of the winning, but when NHRA liberalized rules for 1972 to cater to the kind of compact cars and small-block engines that Detroit was favoring, Pro Stock icon Bill "Grumpy" Jenkins led the charge with the car that revolutionized the class and won the Winternationals in its debut. Grumpy's Toy IX was a Vega hatchback whose chassis used tubular subframes instead of a conventional unibody. It was outfitted with a 331-cid small-block Chevy that reportedly made 600 horsepower, an astronomical figure. Jenkins built on lessons learned from this car and to subsequent versions added components such as the McPherson strut front suspension and dry-sump oiling system that remain standard.

1975: Glidden's Mustang Pro Stocker

In a class in which current-year models aim for Sunday fan loyalty and Monday dealership purchases, Bob Glidden and Ford's Better Idea for 1975 was a five-year-old Mustang. The physical step back was actually a rules-bending step forward because the longer-wheelbase '70 Mustang — which replaced Glidden's all-conquering Pinto — took advantage of a favorable weight break. The Pinto had to carry 7.3 pounds per cubic inch, but the new "old" Mustang, built by Don Hardy, only had to carry 7.1 pounds, an effective weight savings of about 70 pounds. Glidden won the race, his first of a record seven Winternationals triumphs, and the Gatornationals with the car.

1984: Bernstein's Budweiser King Tempo Funny Car

Kenny Bernstein and Dale Armstrong spent the time between the 1983 and 1984 seasons in Ford's Lockheed/Marietta wind tunnel in Georgia refining a new Ford Tempo body. The body sported rounded fenderwells, spoiler lips, enclosed side windows, a rear belly pan, and more and was roughly 10 percent more slippery than the team's 1983 Indy-winning Mercury LN-7. Two months later at the Gatornationals, the car recorded the sport's first 260-mph Funny Car run. The car also featured what was the most sophisticated drag racing onboard computer. Developed by Armstrong and Jim Foust, it monitored and stored the results of an amazing 32 performance functions during a run.

1986: Ormsby's Castrol GTX Streamliner Top Fueler

Aerodynamic trickery certainly was not new to drag racing — many streamlined cars had been attempted in the 1960s — but the 1986 Top Fuel entry of Gary Ormsby and crew chief Lee Beard was as high tech as they came, having been formulated by the best minds of the Indy car racing world using state-of-the-art composites. Ormsby got off to a rough start when ignition wires grounding on the body shell led to blower explosions. The car never ran as fast as it looked, and the idea was shelved after two seasons.

1987: Bernstein's Budweiser King Buick Reatta Funny Car

Three years after rewriting the guidelines for a wind-cheating Funny Car, Kenny Bernstein and Dale Armstrong took the concept to new heights — some might say they took it too far — with a radical-looking Buick LeSabre. Ingloriously dubbed "the Batmobile" and "the dump truck" by its detractors for its huge rear deck, narrow roof, and laid-back windshield, the car was within the letter of the rules but a bit outside the spirit. NHRA worked to close the loopholes for 1988, but there was no arguing with the 1987 car's success: It won the Winternationals and carried Bernstein to his third straight world championship.

2009: Cobra Jets

History repeated itself when the second wave of Ford Cobra Jet factory race cars left an indelible image on the NHRA Winternationals. Forty-one years after their debut in 1968, four new '09 Ford Cobra Jet Mustang factory race cars were unveiled in Pomona by noted car collector Brent Hajek. Each of the new cars, which were driven in Stock by Jimmy Ronzello and former world champions Gary Stinnett, Jim Waldo, and John Calvert, was painted to match the '68-model Cobra Jets campaigned by original Ford factory drivers Al Joniec, Hubert Platt, Gas Rhonda, and Randy Ritchey, who were invited to Pomona for the historic event. Calvert, driving a replica of the Rice-Holman entry that Joniec wheeled to victory in 1968, outlasted 86 other entries to claim the title.

FIRST WINS

The Winternationals is known for firsts, and it was at the season opener in Pomona that many of drag racing's biggest names claimed their first NHRA national event victories. Some were already well on their way to becoming stars; others were just getting started. Not all went on to greatness, and though the following list is by no means all-inclusive, these 16 drivers played a significant role in Winternationals history.

1961
DON NICHOLSON, STOCK

Beginning with this victory, "Dyno Don" Nicholson won eight NHRA national events in three categories (Pro Stock, Modified, and Stock). The versatile Nicholson, who was as adept an engine builder and tuner as he was a driver, surely would have won more had he raced in the 1980s and 1990s instead of the 1960s and 1970s, when there were relatively few NHRA national events. Though most his wins were at match races, Nicholson holds the NHRA record for final-round appearances in the most categories (Funny Car, Pro Stock, Super, Modified, Comp, and Stock).

Utilizing Chevy's new 409-cid engine at the season opener in 1961, Nicholson, driving his recently purchased Impala, and Frank Sanders, in his new Biscayne, both tuned by Nicholson, dominated. After losing a close race to Sanders in the S/S class final the day before, Nicholson turned the tables on Sanders in the Stock final with a 13.59, 105.88. Nicholson defended his title in 1962, and, after switching to a Ford following the 1963 season, was runner-up to Ronnie Sox in Factory Stock in 1964. Nine years later, Nicholson won this third Winternationals title, in Pro Stock.

Arguably the greatest drag racer of all time, "Big Daddy" Don Garlits won his first of 35 NHRA national event titles at the 1963 Winternationals. NHRA had lifted its seven-year nitromethane ban for the event before dropping it forever at both national events the following year, and Garlits couldn't have been happier.

With a wing mounted over the engine, the first on a Top Fuel dragster, Garlits' Swamp Rat V entry attracted considerable attention. Initially rejected, Garlits' winged dragster was allowed to compete, clearing the way for a dominating victory. Not only did Garlits defeat fellow Florida racer Art Malone in the final with an 8.26 at 186.32 mph, but he also set low e.t. at 8.11. Garlits later removed his innovative wing, but he reemployed it eight years later on his first rear-engine car, Swamp Rat XIV, which he debuted with a victory in 1971 at the Winternationals, a race he would win five times.

1963
DON GARLITS, TOP FUEL

1964
RONNIE SOX, FACTORY STOCK

One of the greatest four-speed drivers ever, Ronnie Sox won more races than any Pro Stock competitor during the short-lived four-speed era. He won his first NHRA national event at the 1964 Winternationals against Mercury teammate "Dyno Don" Nicholson, then honed his skills in Super Stock, winning six NHRA national events from 1967 to 1969. The longtime racing partner of Buddy Martin then won nine of 23 NHRA national events from 1970 to 1972, including the 1971 Winternationals.

After running against Martin for several seasons, Sox teamed with his former rival in 1963 and a year later secured a factory deal with Mercury, as did Nicholson, to run one of its new A/FX 427-cid wedge Comets. Mercury built a coupe and a station wagon. Nicholson chose the station wagon, and Sox and Martin wound up with the coupe. The teams met in the final in Pomona, where after losing to Bill Shrewsberry in the A/FX class final on a holeshot, Sox beat Nicholson in the same manner. Sox and Martin capped the season with a trip to England as members of the U.S. Drag Racing Team organized by NHRA.

1965
BILL JENKINS, STOCK

Though best known for his success with Chevys, Pro Stock legend Bill "Grumpy" Jenkins won his first NHRA national event with a Dodge. Jenkins had already made quite a name for himself as a mechanic and tuner. He had teamed with Dave Strickler to win Little eliminator at the 1963 Nationals with an A/FX 427-cid '63 Chevy, and following Chevrolet's exit from racing, the two won class at the 1964 Nationals with their A/FX '64 Dodge. But Jenkins scored his biggest win at the 1965 season opener in his own S/SA Black Arrow '65 Dodge.

Jenkins' Dodge quickened with each round as he made his way through the all-Plymouth field, but his driving made the difference. After defeating Hank Taylor and D.R. Spence, Jenkins left first and ran an 11.41 to beat Bill Shirey's 11.39 in the semifinals, then stopped Dick Housey in the final on another holeshot, 11.39 to 11.37. Jenkins would add three more Winternationals wins to his résumé, including NHRA's first Pro Stock event title in 1970. He scored again in 1972, when he won six of eight NHRA national events, and in 1974, finishing with 13 Pro Stock victories.

1965
DON PRUDHOMME, TOP FUEL

By the time he won this Top Fuel title, Don Prudhomme was well on his way to becoming a legend. Nearly unbeatable in Southern California match races in the feared Greer-Black-Prudhomme entry, Prudhomme hooked up with car owner and crew chief Roland Leong for 1965 and quickly took advantage of the opportunity to showcase his talents on a worldwide stage as the Pomona event was broadcast on ABC's *Wide World of Sports.*

Prudhomme qualified at the top of the 16-car field with a 7.80 at more than 204 mph, just a hundredth ahead of 1963 Winternationals winner "Big Daddy" Don Garlits. Running in the 7.7 range on race day, Prudhomme and the Hawaiian team were unbeatable. Giving up a slight advantage to Bill Alexander in the final, Prudhomme quickly made up the difference and established a clear lead by half-track, running a 7.76 for the first of what would be 49 victories in NHRA national event competition. In an era when supercharged nitro-burning race cars often smoked the tires and were rarely consistent, Prudhomme turned in one of the most impressive performances ever with four runs between 7.75 and 7.87.

1967
CONNIE KALITTA, TOP FUEL

After runner-ups at the 1963 Winternationals in Top Gas and the 1965 Springnationals in Top Fuel, Connie "the Bounty Hunter" Kalitta claimed the first of his 10 NHRA national event Top Fuel titles. Three years earlier, Kalitta had replaced his 392 Hemi with a 427 SOHC Ford and stuck with the once-unworkable combination until by early 1967 he was running better than anyone. Just a week before his NHRA Winternationals victory, Kalitta won the AHRA Winter Nationals in Scottsdale, Ariz., and later that month won the NASCAR Winter Nationals in Daytona Beach, Fla.

Kalitta qualified No. 16, which paired him with No. 32 Chuck Griffith in round one. Kalitta ran a 7.28, the best of the round, and suddenly found himself the favorite. He then defeated Mike Snively with a 7.24 and John Mulligan with a 7.22. In the semifinals, Ford teammate Pete Robinson left first but got out of shape and shut off. Kalitta won easily with a 7.23 to meet Gene Goleman. In a classic Ford versus Chrysler showdown, Goleman slowed to a 7.46, but it's unlikely that he would have been able to match Kalitta's amazing 7.17, 218.43.

1974
LEE SHEPHERD, MODIFIED

Like so many NHRA greats, Lee Shepherd laid the foundation for his remarkable — but all-too-short — Professional career in the Sportsman ranks. Having won the NHRA Division 4 Modified championship in 1973, Shepherd's impressive Winternationals victory the next year was hardly a surprise. Shepherd, who with partners David Reher and Buddy Morrison would dominate Pro Stock in the early 1980s, won 26 of 56 NHRA national events and four world championships from 1980 to 1984.

Driving his partners' Chevy-powered F/Gas Maverick, Shepherd ran back-to-back 10.67s in victories over John Smith's M/Gas Volkswagen and defending event champion Bob Riffle's C/Gas Colt. He stopped Carl Frizzell's E/MP Camaro in the quarterfinals with a 10.66, then held on to beat former Winternationals winner Fred Teixeira's B/Gas Corvette with a 10.49. In the final, Shepherd unleashed a 10.39, 130.62 to set both ends of the F/Gas national record and defeat Jim Marshall's A/MP Dart. Shepherd would win the Winternationals twice in Pro Stock, in 1980 and 1984, and was on his way to a fifth straight Pro Stock championship when he was killed in a testing accident in March 1985.

Mike Edwards made his Pro Stock debut in 1982 at the Winternationals — though he wouldn't compete in Pro Stock again until 1995 — and he won his first NHRA national event at the race a year earlier. Edwards, who had won the Division 4 championship in 1980, pushed his potent B/Super Modified '71 Maverick to runs that were consistently three-tenths under his 10.35 index, but his driving ultimately made the difference.

Like Edwards, fellow Division 4 racer Bill Mansell, who had won the Summernationals and Cajun Nationals in 1979, had bettered his 9.50 index by as much as three-tenths en route to the final. Driving the Mansell, Minga & Suski D/Gas Monza, Mansell did better than that against Edwards, running a 9.07 on his 9.50 index. But it was all for naught as Edwards took the win with a better reaction time and a 10.00. Edwards would win the Mile-High Nationals that year, but he wouldn't win again until 1996, when he won three races and finished third in his first full season in Pro Stock.

1981
MIKE EDWARDS, MODIFIED

1984
GARY ORMSBY, TOP FUEL

In 1989, Gary Ormsby used his Winternationals victory as a springboard to the NHRA Top Fuel world championship. It was his first of six NHRA national event victories that season, but it wasn't his first in Pomona. Five years earlier, Ormsby had won the first of 14 NHRA Top Fuel titles at the season opener, defeating Joe Amato in the first of what would be many final-round meetings between them before Ormsby's career was cut short by cancer in 1991.

Ormsby, who in 1983 won the *Popular Hot Rodding* Championships and was runner-up at the Golden Gate Nationals in his first NHRA national event final, got off to a shaky start when his dragster lost the rear wing on his first qualifying run. Ormsby qualified No. 4 and in the first round made the quickest run of his career, a 5.52, to dispose of Dick LaHaie. He then beat Gene Snow and Larry Minor — who shook the tires and slowed to a 5.74 after setting low e.t. of the meet (5.40) in the previous round — before taking a narrow 5.66 to 5.67 victory over Amato, who would beat Ormsby in a final-round rematch the following year.

1990
LORI JOHNS, TOP FUEL

After three semifinal finishes in 1989 in her first full season in Top Fuel, 24-year-old Lori Johns kicked off her sophomore campaign with a stunning victory. Johns became just the third woman to win an NHRA national event Top Fuel title when she drove past four of drag racing's biggest stars — Eddie Hill, Don Prudhomme, Kenny Bernstein, and Dick LaHaie — veterans who were making their marks on the sport long before she was born.

Johns qualified No. 6 with a 5.02 and ran 5.04 and 5.08 in victories over Hill and Prudhomme, respectively. She got the only break she needed in the semifinals when Bernstein red-lighted and shut off after launching into a big wheelstand. Johns steamed downtrack but lost the blower belt at about 1,000 feet and coasted to a 5.22. In the final, Johns and LaHaie left together and finished nearly as closely, with Johns eking out a five-thousandths victory against the former world champion, 5.031 to 5.035. With her victory, Johns joined 18-time winner Shirley Muldowney and 1982 Southern Nationals champion Lucille Lee as the only women in NHRA history to win a national event in Top Fuel.

1990
K.C. SPURLOCK, FUNNY CAR

After two decades, Funny Car rookie K.C. Spurlock's win remains one of the biggest upsets in NHRA history. Spurlock, the son of well-known country-music promoter C.K. Spurlock, made the jump to nitro racing after less than a year behind the wheel of a Top Alcohol Funny Car. He received his NHRA Funny Car license just nine days before the start of the 1990 season and defeated four established drivers to take a most unlikely victory.

Under the guidance of crew chief Ronnie Swearingen, Spurlock qualified his Ford Probe on the bump for the tough 16-car field, then advanced through eliminations with wins over low qualifier John Force, R.C. Sherman, and reigning world champion Bruce Larson. Spurlock's defeat of Force was perhaps the most shocking as Force had run a 5.28 to lead qualifying and had outrun Spurlock in all four sessions. In the final, Ed "the Ace" McCulloch, who had set low e.t. of the meet with a 5.27, smoked the tires, allowing Spurlock to cruise to the win, recording an off-pace 5.78 when his blower belt broke at half-track.

1991
RICK SANTOS, TOP ALCOHOL DRAGSTER

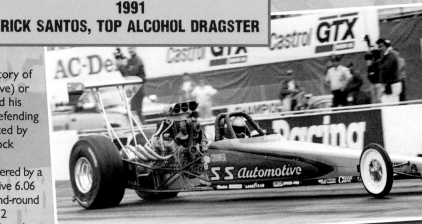

Though he never raced as a Professional, Rick Santos' accomplishments in NHRA's highly competitive Top Alcohol Dragster category are second to none. No driver in the history of the class has won more national championships (five) or more national events (36) than Santos, who scored his first by defeating reigning national and two-time defending event champion Blaine Johnson. In a class dominated by big-inch hemi-powered machines, Santos' small-block Chevy-powered entry was a popular winner.

Santos qualified his S&S Automotive dragster, powered by a 376-cid Chevy, No. 6 with a 6.13, then ran an impressive 6.06 to defeat Jim Rizzoli in round one. After an easy second-round win over a tire-rattling Jim Scott, Santos defeated No. 2 qualifier Stephen Fedele in the semifinals, 6.06 to 6.09, and won the final when Johnson, who had qualified No. 1 with a 6.02 and set low e.t. in round one with a 5.97, red-lighted. Santos also won the Auto Club NHRA Finals that year and three national events in 1993, including the prestigious Mac Tools U.S. Nationals, before parking his machine prior to the 1996 season. He drove for Jack O'Bannon from 1996 until his retirement in 2002 and won five consecutive championships (1997-2001).

1997
GARY SCELZI, TOP FUEL

Gary Scelzi's first Top Fuel victory helped launch a fantastic Professional career that would include four NHRA world championships (three in Top Fuel and one in Funny Car) and more than 40 national event victories. Scelzi got his racing start at sand-drag events, then switched to asphalt, on which he won the 1985 Auto Club NHRA Finals in Top Alcohol Dragster. A close friend of the Johnson family, Scelzi was a natural choice to drive Alan Johnson's Top Fuel car following the death of Blaine Johnson in 1996.

It didn't take long for Scelzi to get acclimated to his new surroundings, and he qualified No. 1 in Pomona and cruised to the final with wins against Spike Gorr, Connie Kalitta, and Cory McClenathan. Paired with Joe Amato in the title round, Scelzi got the best of the five-time champion. Though few had questioned Johnson's choice, Scelzi left little doubt that he was the right person for the job by winning again two weeks later in Phoenix. By the end of his rookie season, Scelzi had appeared in 10 final rounds and recorded five wins and was crowned the NHRA Top Fuel world champion.

1998
JACK BECKMAN, SUPER COMP

Jack Beckman has yet to win the Winternationals as a Professional, but he won it twice as a Sportsman racer. Beckman, who won the 2003 Super Comp national championship before landing his first nitro ride two years later, won his first NHRA national event behind the wheel of Dennis and Jim Gorney's dragster. The Gorneys, who had bought the car from Beckman's partner Brent Cannon, loaned the car to Beckman to use at the Winternationals after his dragster was destroyed in a crash the previous season.

Making the most of his opportunity, Beckman ran an 8.91 on the class' 8.90 index to beat Luke Shumard in round three, then scored a pivotal fourth-round win against Martin Rouse. After identical reaction times, Beckman won that race in a double breakout, 8.88 to 8.86. He won his quarterfinal race when Michael Peck red-lighted and in the semifinals ran a dead-on 8.90 to beat Rick Beckstrom's too quick 8.86. In an extremely close final, Beckman was slightly slower off the line but hit the stripe just ahead of Tommy Phillips, 8.95 to 8.96. Beckman would win the Winternationals again in 2003.

Following a legend is never easy, but soft-spoken Texan Darrell Russell handled the job perfectly when he won in his debut as the driver for Joe Amato. The five-time NHRA Top Fuel champ and winner of more than 50 national events chose Russell as his successor following his sudden retirement in 2000. Like Gary Scelzi, Russell had extensive experience in a supercharged Top Alcohol Dragster, but he had never handled a four-second, 300-mph nitroburner.

2001
DARRELL RUSSELL, TOP FUEL

His experience was never an issue. Russell qualified well, then calmly motored through eliminations with wins against Andrew Cowin, Doug Kalitta, and Bobby Baldwin. Paired with Mike Dunn in the final, Russell scored with a 4.65 after Dunn smoked the tires. Russell was invited to take Amato's place in the NHRA Shootout bonus race, which had been postponed from the 1996 season finale in Pomona. Racing against seven of the sport's best, Russell looked right at home as he advanced to the final before losing to friend and mentor Scelzi. That year, he won two races and posted a very respectable sixth-place finish. Sadly, he was killed in a racing accident in 2004, cutting short a very promising career.

A two-time national event winner in Top Alcohol Dragster, second-generation racer Melanie Troxel became the sixth woman to win an NHRA national event Top Fuel title. A two-time runner-up in parts of four seasons from 2000 to 2005 (she didn't compete in 2001 or 2004), Troxel advanced to the final at five straight races to begin the season — a Top Fuel record — and scored two wins; she would lead the points through the first 12 races and post a career-best fourth-place finish.

After losing to teammate Tony Schumacher in the title round at the 2005 season finale, Troxel returned to Pomona and, after destroying an engine in the first round against Clay Millican, defeated Schumacher in the second round in the class' best race, 4.52 to 4.53. She turned back Morgan Lucas in the semifinals with a 4.55 and won the final easily over a tire-spinning David Baca with a 4.58. Troxel won again four races later in Las Vegas and would win twice more in Top Fuel in 2007 before switching to Funny Car in 2008, when she would become the second woman to win an NHRA national event in that category.

2006
MELANIE TROXEL, TOP FUEL

FROM PARKING LOT TO SUPER TRACK

The story of Pomona Raceway, renamed Auto Club Raceway at Pomona in 2006, essentially mirrors the history of organized hot rodding: Responsibly minded members of car clubs joined forces with foresighted civic and law-enforcement officials to replace dangerous street racing with sanctioned competition at designated sites.

Street racing was a serious epidemic in the late 1940s. Chuck Griffith, then the president of Choppers Car Club, which became the Pomona Valley Timing Association (PVTA), said, "We had several friends who were killed in street racing accidents, and our club was real serious about getting everyone off the streets. When I first met Pomona Police Chief Ralph Parker, he was a regular motorcycle officer in the late 1940s, and he knew who the racers were and was giving them a lot of tickets. Parker found out about our club meetings, and he began sending another Pomona police officer, Bud Coons [who would later become a member of the original NHRA Safety Safari], as an emissary to our meetings."

The Choppers began holding organized races in Fontana in late 1950 but, because of the windy area, relocated to the L.A. County Fairgrounds in 1951. "The Pomona Police Department and the Fairgrounds officials worked together on many things, and it was their decision to use part of their property as a place for us to stage our races."

The Choppers became incorporated as the PVTA because the group's accountant thought it would be a good idea if the organization was going to be working with civic officials. PVTA began using timing equipment produced by J. Otto Crocker, who also worked with NHRA founder Wally Parks and the fledgling organization, which was holding time-trial events in the desert. "That's how Wally found out about us," said Griffith. "He began stopping by our races at Fontana and then Pomona. When NHRA decided to become more involved with drag racing, all of the car clubs met with Wally at Bakersfield to formulate the rules for his new sanctioning body."

Races began to be held at Pomona Raceway, and

Competitors were not allowed to make runs on the track until their cars had undergone a stringent tech inspection by PVTA members.

(Above left) The Pomona Valley Timing Association (PVTA), in conjunction with the Pomona Police Department and civic and L.A. County Fairgrounds officials, began conducting organized drag races at the Fairgrounds parking lot in 1951. This is the first NHRA sanctioned race, held April 11-12, 1953. Among the early landmarks was the pump tower on the top end. (Above right) Classic post-World War II hot rods filled the staging lanes during early events. It's a safe bet that most competitors were former street racers who had been convinced that organized competition was the way to go.

trophies were given to the eliminator winners and war bonds to the Top Eliminator winner. PVTA worked with Fairgrounds manager Phil Shepard. "They helped us with many things, such as equipment, along with painters, electricians, etc.," said Griffith.

In addition to providing an organized format for the events, PVTA dealt with many outside parties. "We had to answer to Chief Parker, the Pomona City Council, the Fairgrounds, and, of course, the city of La Verne, which had a lot of local churches in the area. We did whatever we could do to make them like us, not hate us, and for the most part, it worked out real well."

NHRA held its first sanctioned races in Pomona in 1953 and 1954, and when it came time for the first NHRA Winternationals in 1961, six years after the first NHRA Nationals had been conducted in Great Bend, Kan., no one was surprised that Pomona Raceway was chosen as the host track. "Wally always had a real fondness for Pomona," recalled Griffith.

"It's like you always remember your first car. Pomona was Wally's first dragstrip, and no matter how much more modern the other ones became, Pomona was always Wally's favorite."

Griffith said that it didn't take much persuasion by NHRA to convince local officials of the many benefits of staging the Winternationals. "Wally presented it to them in terms of dollars and cents, citing how many people would be coming in from out of town and how much they would be spending for food and lodging. And, of course, it would further our original goal of getting the kids off the streets. There really wasn't much resistance."

Of all the tracks on the NHRA schedule, none is located so deeply within a city. That the Winternationals is celebrating its 50th anniversary where acres of orange groves have given way to massive housing and commercial developments is a great testament to all who have helped organize and/or participated in this great event for the last half century.

This view of the starting line looking north shows the many citrus packing houses that used to populate La Verne, required to handle the annual spring harvest of the orange groves along Foothill Boulevard and in surrounding areas during the 1950s.

This 1950s overhead view shows that even the earliest events attracted many participants and spectators. Note the iconic lineup of Italian Cypress trees. The only sign of any development was Brackett Field airport, which still operates.

(Above) By 1960, just one year before the Winternationals was first held, many of drag racing's pioneering stars competed in Pomona, including Doug Cook's Howard Cams '40 Studebaker, far lane, and Junior Thompson's '41 Studebaker. At this Southwest divisional meet, Cook reset the C/GS record to 12.08, 116.73. (Left) NHRA held its second sanctioned event in Pomona in 1954. Participants signed in and received souvenir pins from PVTA at the NHRA mobile headquarters unit, which would become the famous Safety Safari trailer that went on its first of many national tours that summer.

The white banner stretching over the starting line at the first Winternationals in 1961 was the original in a long line of evolving and well-recognized versions.

(Above) NHRA founder Wally Parks, left, appreciated the use of professional graphics to promote a positive, organized image. The Winternationals banners were hand-lettered, in this instance for the 1963 event by an artist from local business Sign Art. (Right) In 1969, Pomona Police Chief Ralph Parker, who played a pivotal role in helping establish the annual event, was honored by Parks and NHRA at a ceremony before eliminations. The dragstrip was officially dubbed Parker Avenue with a Pomona street sign anchored to the left of the starting line. Miss Winternationals Marsha Bennett joined Parks for the presentation. In 2007, Parks was honored with a street sign designating the staging lanes Wally Parks Blvd.

As the event grew, more timing towers were added, including this one behind the starting line in addition to the tower just east of the starting line.

(Above) The old made way for the new in 1993, and the facility was completely overhauled. Permanent grandstands were erected on both sides of the track, and the centerpiece was a tower-suites complex that formed part of the sound wall that wraps around the starting-line area. (Left) The facility is known for possessing one of the most picturesque backdrops of any track. The timing of the Winternationals certainly doesn't hurt; the San Gabriel Mountains are typically covered with snow from the top of Mount Baldy to the base of the foothills just in time for the event. These 1970s grandstands were enormous but temporary; at the conclusion of each event, they were disassembled so that the area could be used as fairgrounds parking.

A CHANGING LANDSCAPE

The Winternationals snowflake became one of the most iconic logos of an NHRA national event, and from 1963 until 1993, the symbol was displayed on the starting-line banner. When extensive renovations were completed in 1993, the banner was retired because it blocked the view from the tower suites.

(Left) An early landmark was the Italian Cypress trees along what is now known as Fairplex Drive and along the turnoff. When racers shut off their engines and were slowing after the finish line, the trees were easily caught in their peripheral vision, and there was no mistaking that they were in Pomona. (Below) The two-story timing tower on the west side of the property, shown in 1978, was the main building for many years. It was demolished in 1993.

Auto Club Raceway at Pomona is a far cry from its humble beginnings and remains a celebrated location for the NHRA Full Throttle Drag Racing Series season opener.

Auto Club Raceway at Pomona, on the west side of Fairplex at Pomona, has been the site of the season-opening Kragen O'Reilly NHRA Winternationals since the first event in 1961. The facility, nestled in the foothills of the picturesque San Gabriel Mountains, is the oldest destination on the NHRA Full Throttle Drag Racing Series tour, and it is steeped in history, having been the proving ground for new technology and the backdrop for many debuts since opening its doors to the racing community.

The history of the facility began long before the inaugural Winternationals — the first sanctioned race was held there in 1953 — but since the esteemed event has been held at the Pomona track, the facility has undergone vast improvements. A makeshift timing tower was replaced with a permanent, though small, version in 1968 and later upgraded to an expansive, state-of-the-art building that includes corporate suites and an impressive media center.

In addition, temporary seating was replaced with permanent grandstands, followed by a repaving of the racing surface, which included an extension of the concrete launchpad to 660 feet, and the installation of luxury VIP box suites along the top of the eastern grandstands.

Though many changes have improved Auto Club Raceway at Pomona, one fact remains the same: The revered facility is the scenic setting for two of the most highly anticipated events each season, the season-opening Kragen O'Reilly NHRA Winternationals and the season-closing Automobile Club of Southern California NHRA Finals.

THE WINTERNATIONALS
by the Numbers

MOST WINS (ALL CLASSES)

1. **Bob Glidden** (Pro Stock) 7
2. **Don Garlits** (Top Fuel) 5
   Warren Johnson (Pro Stock) 5
   Don Prudhomme (Top Fuel, Funny Car) 5
   Rick Santos (Top Alcohol Dragster) 5
6. **Greg Anderson** (Pro Stock) 4
   John Force (Funny Car) 4
   Bill Jenkins (Pro Stock) 4
   Gary Scelzi (Top Fuel, Funny Car,
   Top Alcohol Dragster) 4
10. **Pat Austin** (Top Alcohol Funny Car) 3
    Tony Bartone (Top Alcohol Dragster,
    Top Alcohol Funny Car) 3
    Bill Bushmaker (Stock) 3
    John Calvert (Super Stock, Stock) 3
    Gordon Collett (Top Gas) 3
    Larry Dixon Jr. (Top Fuel) 3
    Dan Fletcher (Comp, Super Stock) 3
    Frank Iaconio (Pro Stock) 3
    Frank Manzo (Top Alcohol Funny Car) 3
    Don Nicholson (Pro Stock, Stock) 3
    Cruz Pedregon (Funny Car, Top Alcohol
    Dragster, Top Alcohol Funny Car) 3
    Al Segrini (Funny Car) 3
    Lee Shepherd (Pro Stock, Modified) 3
    Bobby Taylor (Top Alcohol Dragster) 3
    Larry Tores (Comp, Super Stock) 3
    Hugh Tucker (Sportsman, Jr., Little) 3
    Jim Waldo (Stock) 3
    Ron Zoelle (Super Stock) 3

MOST TOP FUEL WINS

1. **Don Garlits**   5
2. **Larry Dixon Jr.**   3
3. **Joe Amato**   2
   Frank Bradley   2
   Dick LaHaie   2
   Shirley Muldowney   2
   Gary Ormsby Sr.   2
   Gary Scelzi   2
   Tony Schumacher   2

MOST FUNNY CAR WINS

1. **John Force** 4
   Don Prudhomme 4
3. **Al Segrini** 3
4. **Ron Capps** 2
   Robert Hight 2
   Tony Pedregon 2
   Dale Pulde 2
   K.C. Spurlock 2
   Jerry Toliver 2

MOST PRO STOCK WINS

1. **Bob Glidden** 7
2. **Warren Johnson** 5
3. **Greg Anderson** 4
   Bill Jenkins 4
5. **Frank Iaconio** 3
6. **Darrell Alderman** 2
   Jeg Coughlin 2
   Jerry Eckman 2
   Lee Shepherd 2
   Jim Yates 2

MOST PRO FINAL ROUNDS

1. **Warren Johnson** (Pro Stock).......................11
2. **Bob Glidden** (Pro Stock) 8
3. **John Force** (Funny Car)...............................7
   Don Prudhomme (Top Fuel, Funny Car).....7
5. **Joe Amato** (Top Fuel) 6
   Kenny Bernstein (Top Fuel, Funny Car).......6
   Don Garlits (Top Fuel) 6
8. **Frank Iaconio** (Pro Stock).............................5
9. **Darrell Alderman** (Pro Stock) 4
   Greg Anderson (Pro Stock)..........................4
   Raymond Beadle (Funny Car) 4
   Jeg Coughlin (Pro Stock) 4
   Larry Dixon Jr. (Top Fuel) 4
   Jim Head (Top Fuel, Funny Car) 4
   Connie Kalitta (Top Fuel)..............................4
   Tony Pedregon (Funny Car) 4
   Dale Pulde (Funny Car)................................4
   Jim Yates (Pro Stock) 4

LONGEST WINNING STREAKS

1. **Don Prudhomme**....... 4 (Funny Car: 1975-78)
2. **Greg Anderson** .... 3 (Pro Stock: 2006-08)
3. **Jeg Coughlin** .... 2 (Pro Stock: 1999-2000)
   Larry Dixon Jr. .... 2 (Top Fuel: 2002-03)
   Bob Glidden........... 2 (Pro Stock: 1978-79)
   Bob Glidden........... 2 (Pro Stock: 1975-76)
   Frank Iaconio .... 2 (Pro Stock: 1982-83)
   Warren Johnson .... 2 (Pro Stock: 1993-94)
   Al Segrini .... 2 (Funny Car: 1984-85)

FAMILIES WITH MULTIPLE PRO WINNERS

Dixon: Larry Sr. and Larry Jr.
Johnson: Warren and Kurt
Kalitta: Connie, Scott, and Doug
Pedregon: Cruz and Tony
Schumacher: Don and Tony

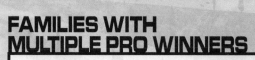
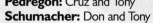

WINTERNATIONALS WINNERS · 1961-2009

Seven Times
Bob Glidden

Five Times
Don Garlits
Warren Johnson
Don Prudhomme
Rick Santos

Four Times
Greg Anderson
John Force
Bill Jenkins
Gary Scelzi

Three Times
Pat Austin
Tony Bartone
Bill Bushmaker
John Calvert
Gordon Collett
Larry Dixon Jr.
Dan Fletcher
Frank Iaconio
Frank Manzo
Don Nicholson
Cruz Pedregon
Al Segrini
Lee Shepherd
Bobby Taylor
Larry Tores

Hugh Tucker
Jim Waldo
Ron Zoelle

Two Times
Darrell Alderman
Joe Amato
Brad Anderson
Bucky Austin
Chuck Beal
Jack Beckman
Kenny Bernstein
Dave Boertman
Frank Bradley
Chico Breschini
Ron Capps

Al Corda
Jeg Coughlin
Randy Daniels
Jimmy DeFrank
Jerry Eckman
Don Enriquez
Mark Faul
Phil Featherston
Steve Federlin
Mike Ferderer
Ron Filkins
Lou Gasparrelli
Sheldon Gecker
Val Hedworth
Robert Hight
Blaine Johnson

Randy Jones
Scott Kendig
Dick LaHaie
Dick Landy
Toby Lang
Butch Leal
John Lingenfelter
Don Little
Abe Loewen
Shirley Muldowney
Bob Newberry
Gary Ormsby
Jay Payne
Tony Pedregon
Barrie Poole
Jeff Powers

Dale Pulde
Scotty Richardson
Coleman Roddy
Tony Schumacher
Kyle Seipel
Duane Shields
Ronnie Sox
K.C. Spurlock
Steve Taylor
Jerry Toliver
Steve Woods
Jim Yates
Les Young

One Time
Paul Alabab
Jeb Allen
Randy Anderson
Shelly Anderson
David Andrews
Dale Armstrong
Harry Axemaker
"Bones" Balough
John Barkley
Bill Barney
Gary Beck
David Benisek
Bill Bennett
Gene Bichlmeier
Mike Blodgett
Ron Bonfanti
Richard Bourgeois
Doug Bracey
Brooks Brown
Don Brown
Kelly Brown
Bob Button
Gary Cagle
Dean Carter
Anthony Castillo
Carroll Caudle
Richard Charbon-
neau
Arnold Chaves
Jack Chrisman
Tony Christian
Wayne Clapp
Marcel Cloutier
David Coapstick
Mark Coletti
Dave Connolly
Doug Cook
Gary Cooke

Wiley Cossey
Jim Cowan
Don Cumby
Bernie Cunning-
ham
Al DaPozzo
Jerry Darien
Mike DePalma
Ed DeStaute
Jack Ditmars
Larry Dixon Sr.
Ken Dondero
Graham Douglas
Mike Dunn
Ernie Dutre
Al Ekstrand
Mike Edwards
Bob Elliott
Dale Emery
Jim Epler
Randy Fabbro
Dennis Ferrara
Lou Ficco Jr.
Les Figueroa
Alan Fillebrown
Alan Freese
Rich Galli
John Geyer
Jeff Gillette
Doug Gordon
Dave Grassi
Tim Grose
Don Grotheer
Tommy Grove
Darrell Gwynn
Dave Hage
Don Hampton
Bob Harris Jr.
Rod Hartzell

Jerry Harvey
Frank Hawley
Bob Herr
Mike Hiatt
Eddie Hill
Vic Hobbs
Al Hofmann
Clark Holroyd
Tom Hoover
Rick Houser
John Hyland
Duane Jacobsen
Lori Johns
Brandon Johnson
Hank Johnson
Kurt Johnson
Tommy Johnson Jr.
Al Joniec
Connie Kalitta
Doug Kalitta
Scott Kalitta
Ted Kellner
Rick Kelly
Dave Kempton
Ed Kohler
Larry Kopp
Justin Lamb
Bob Lambeck
Jeff Lane
Jody Lang
Chad Langdon
Bruce Larson
Bo Laws
Bill Lawton
Jimmy Lewis
Judy Lilly
Jason Line
Jeff Lion
Smylie Little

Mike Loge
Larry Lombardo
Johnny Loper
Denny Lucas
Keith Lynch
Butch Maas
Dick Manz
George Marnell
Bill Maropulos
Kip Martin
Jerry McClanahan
Kevin McClelland
Ed McCulloch
Bruce McDowell
Jim Meador
Jim Mederer
Dave Meredith
Billy Meyer
Jim Meyer
Dave Meziere
Larry Miner
Kenny Moore
Bryan Morrison
John Mulligan
Pat Mulligan
Bob Muravez
Mitch Myers
Tony Nancy
Jim Nelson
Bo Nickens
Buddy Nickens
David Nickens
Jimmy Nix
Bob Noice
Carl Olson
Danny Ongais
Bob Panella Jr.
Steve Parsons
Ken Passerby

Allan Patterson
Todd Patterson
Gary Pearman
Art Peterson
Chuck Phelps
Brad Pierce
Bernie Plourd
Chuck Rayburn
Brian Raymer
Larry Reyes
Tom Ridings
Bob Riffle
Rob Robinson
Ron Root
Marvin Rouse
Darrell Russell
Jerry Ruth
Clare Sanders
Bruce Sarver
Larry Scarth
Ed Schuck Jr.
Don Schumacher
Ted Seipel
Ed Sellnow
Dave Settles
Joey Severance
Shirley Shahan
John Shoemaker
Ed Sigmon
Charlie Smith
Greg Smith

Paul Smith
Mike Snively
Gene Snow
Jim Stevens
Walt Stevens
Michael Stone
Dick St. Peter
Shane Studley
Gary Sutton
Dennis Taylor
Fred Teixeira
Tom Tereau
Mickey Thompson
Bob Tietz
J.R. Todd
Val Torres Jr.
Melanie Troxel
Mike Troxel
Tom Turner
Eddie Vasquez
Ken Veney
Earl Wade
Eric Waldo
James Warren
John Weaver
Jim Whiteley
Dick Whitman
Dean Whittman
Jack Williams
Richard Wood
Tom Yancer

CPSIA information can be obtained
at www.ICGtesting.com
Printed in the USA
LVIC06n1235081213
364398LV00014B/160